W9-CYH-016

What Good Parents Have in Common

Thirteen
Secrets for
Success

What
Good
Parents
Have in
Common

Janis Long Harris

ZondervanPublishingHouse
Grand Rapids, Michigan

A Division of HarperCollinsPublishers

What Good Parents Have in Common
Copyright © 1994 by Janis Long Harris

Requests for information should be directed to:
Zondervan Publishing House
Grand Rapids, Michigan 49530

Library of Congress Cataloging-in-Publication Data

Harris, Janis Long, 1951–
    What good parents have in common : thirteen secrets for success /
Janis Long Harris.
        p. cm.
    ISBN 0-310-48191-0 (pbk.)
    1. Parenting. 2. Child rearing. I. Title.
HQ755.8.H37   1994
649'.1—dc20   93-41052
                                                                  CIP

All Scripture quotations, unless otherwise noted, are taken from the *Holy Bible: New International Version* (North American Edition). Copyright © 1973, 1978, 1984, by the International Bible Society. Used by permission of Zondervan Bible Publishers.

All rights reserved. No part of this publication may be reproduced, stored in a retrieval system, or transmitted in any form or by any means—electronic, mechanical, photocopy, recording, or any other—except for brief quotations in printed reviews, without the prior permission of the publisher.

Edited by Linda Vanderzalm
Cover design by Dennis Hill
Cover photo copyright © by Walter Hodges/West Light

Printed in the United States of America

94 95 96 97 98 / DH / 5 4 3 2 1

For my parents

Contents

Introduction

[Their] children arise and call [them] blessed.

Proverbs 31:28

WHAT PARENTS don't hope for a day when their children will "call them blessed"? Unfortunately, nobody seems to do that anymore. Walk through any bookstore and read the titles. Listen to the conversations at any party. Watch any television talk show. These days, unhappy adult children seem to be blaming their parents for everything from alcoholism to failure in love to career problems. It seems that we live in a nation full of "toxic" parents, that most of us came from dysfunctional families.

As the parent of two young children, I take all this negativity personally. And I worry. Books, magazine articles, and television specials abound about the myriad ways parents can permanently traumatize their children. Take your children to church, teach them spiritual values, and you've "crammed religion down their throats." Discipline your children, and you've "repressed" them. Be too permissive, and they'll become insecure. Teach them to work, and you've robbed them of their childhood. Love them too much, and you've spoiled them.

Although some of the admonitions about potentially harmful forms of parenting may be partially true, they're not very helpful to me. I need encouragement, not dire warnings. I seek models to follow, not examples of failure to shun. I want people to help me raise healthy children: children who will grow up with strong self-esteem, who will understand and apply their gifts so they can find satisfying work, who will have the capacity to love others, who will embrace strong ethical and spiritual values. I want to find out what common denominators characterize good parents—not those that define "bad" parents.

Tolstoy said that all happy families are alike, while unhappy families are unhappy in their own way. I undertook this book with the assumption that, like happy families, good parents are in many ways alike. I wanted to know the essential ingredients of good parenting—the attitudes and actions that make children rise up and call their parents blessed.

One fact is clear: the experts disagree about what makes for good parenting. I've heard experts expound philosophies ranging from "love is all they need" to "tough love," from "say yes whenever you can" to "be sure to give them ample doses of healthy frustration."

Despite their sometimes conflicting advice, the professionals can be very helpful. I've benefited tremendously from the books of several well-known child-development specialists. But I've also benefited from another category of expert: adult children of good parents, adult children who have experienced the satisfactions and benefits of effective parenting.

What is the definition of a good parent? For the purposes of this book, a good parent is one whose adult child shows evidence of strong character and a sense of well-being, has a capacity for work and love, believes he or she had good parents, and consequently has a desire to rise up and call them blessed.

In writing this book, I interviewed people of strong character and high achievement, people whose parents fit this description. I asked them to describe their childhood home and their parents' strengths. Almost everyone I interviewed assured me that their parents weren't perfect—hardly a surprise—and then went on to describe them in remarkably loving terms.

In the process of listening to their stories, I began to see some strong trends emerging. Some fit my preconceptions, others didn't. Some really surprised me—such as the ways good parents discipline their kids. I became convinced that while good parents can differ greatly in many ways, they have some definite characteristics in common. This books attempts to portray those characteristics through the stories and reflections of scores of adult children.

For the most part, I've let the interviewees speak for themselves. As a result, this book is more an oral history told by children of good parents than it is a summary of my own thoughts and conclusions about childrearing, although there's some of that too. Each chapter of the book deals with a different trait of good parents as perceived by their grown children. The concluding chapter gives some suggestions about how to use the information contained in the preceding pages.

Because I interviewed several dozen adult children, it was impossible to tell all their stories. Each, however, provided valuable insight into what goes into effective parenting and helped me tremendously by adding to the anecdotal data bank that I eventually sorted into thirteen characteristics of good parents. You may recognize the names of some of the adult children I interviewed: Mary Kay Ash, Luis Palau, Madeleine L'Engle, Jay Kesler, Timothy Johnson, Grace Ketterman, Joan Beck, Ben Carson, Fred Barnes, and Donald Cole, for instance. Although you may not recognize the names of the others, they too are people whose ability to love and work and serve is in part a gift from their unusually effective parents.

I want to be an effective parent. In sharing their memories and insights, in telling their stories, the people I interviewed for this book have given me pictures and tools to help me become a better parent. And perhaps my children one day will rise up and call me blessed. Perhaps yours someday will too.

·ONE·

Encourage Your Children

I always felt my parents were so proud of me, that they admired me. The feeling I used to get was that anything I did, they thought was great.

Luis Palau

My mother thought I was super. Mother thought I was the best thing ever invented. We all grew up with a great sense of security because we were constantly affirmed.

Donald Cole

MARY KAY ASH, founder and chairwoman of Mary Kay Cosmetics, built her multi-million-dollar company on a principle she learned from her mother—a principle that is, to an astonishingly consistent degree, characteristic of good parents.

Ash *encourages* her employees into succeeding, just as her mother encouraged her. "One of the reasons we're successful is the fact that we praise people to success," she explains. "That's what my parents, especially my mother, did for me. I think criticism is destructive. It damages people's self-esteem and causes them to be resentful. We tell our managers that if

13

they must level criticism—and occasionally you must—sandwich it in between two heavy layers of praise. I've carried that over from my mother, and I feel it's very important. I have great expectations for women. I constantly encourage them to do the things I know they can do if they put their hearts and minds to it."

Ash's mother had great expectations of her, and she empowered her to fulfill those expectations with a blizzard of encouragement. "I had an unusual childhood," Ash explains. "My father was an invalid, and since my mother had to work to support us, I took care of him from the time I was seven years old."

As the family's sole wage-earner, Ash's mother had to work seven days a week at her job as a restaurant manager in order to make ends meet. She left the house at 5:00 in the morning and came home at 9:00 at night. For years, she was out of the house before her daughter got up and didn't get back until she was already in bed. Consequently, young Ash's main contact with her mother was by telephone.

"I called her any time I needed help," recalls Ash. "I'd call and say, 'Mother, Daddy wants this or that for dinner. How do I do it?' And she'd tell me in great detail. And she'd end each conversation with, 'Honey, Mother knows you can do it.'

"'You can do it' became my middle name," Ash continues. "She would encourage me to do anything in the world I set my heart on. She'd say, 'Of course you can do it.' I became an honor scholar because of her encouragement and praise. She wasn't a mother who stayed home and baked cookies—she was never at home—but I called her all day long. And those phone conversations were bright spots in my day. I always knew that if I felt down in the mouth, she would lift me up. She was a fantastic encourager, one of the greatest encouragers who ever lived."

Encouragement is one of the traits grown children of good

parents cite most frequently as characteristic of their parents. Their parents encouraged them through verbal affirmation, practical help, visualizing success, presence, recognition of individual strengths, support without pressure, unconditional approval, and expectations.

VERBAL AFFIRMATION

Good parents encourage their children with words. "My parents complimented me all the time," recalls evangelist Luis Palau. "It wasn't a psychological thing; they just did it. Sometimes I'll look in the mirror and say, 'You know, you're pretty ugly,' but my parents always made me feel I was very handsome. I used to feel, 'Man, am I good looking!' And I remember when I started reading my first words, everybody was giggling and applauding. I thought, *Wow! Reading is a big deal around here!*"

Mary O'Connor, now a mother of four, believes the seeds of her confidence in her current role were sown by her father's encouraging words: "He would say to me, 'You're going to make somebody a good wife,' or, 'You're going to be a good mother.' That made me feel I could be successful at this."

Good parents know that some of their most powerfully encouraging words are those that their children overhear. "One of my greatest memories," says Taylor University President Jay Kesler, "is of being taken to the stores as a little boy. I would be hanging on my dad's finger, I must have been about four or five, and he would always introduce me and say something nice about me. His friends would say something obligatory like, 'You have a nice son,' and he would say, 'Yes, he's a good boy. We're very proud of him.' I always liked that."

Child psychiatrist and pediatrician Grace Ketterman has similar memories: "My mother would sometimes nag me about things," she says, "but then she would brag about me when I did a good job. When she would tell people how well I had done something, it felt really good."

The Most Valuable Affirmation

Good parents know that the most effective compliment is a hard-earned one. Cheap praise, like cheap grace, isn't worth much. Nancy Swider-Peltz' dad knew that, and his knowledge probably influenced her development as an Olympic speed-skater. As a young girl, Swider-Peltz was a natural athlete, and she loved participating in sports, but there's little question she pushed herself to excel in part because she wanted to hear those hard-won words of affirmation from her dad. "My father was extremely reserved with compliments," she muses. "They were few and far between. But when he said something positive, it felt so good. We understood we had to work hard for Dad's compliments, and I respected and liked that so much."

In attempting to make their praise rare enough to be valuable, parents face the danger of going too far the other way. Kids are easily discouraged if they feel it's next to impossible to please their parents. As much as she appreciated her father's approach to praise, Swider-Peltz admits that his infrequent compliments might not have been enough if her mother hadn't been freer in her commendations. Swider-Peltz' mother wasn't given to empty praise, but she tended to give her children compliments on a more regular basis than did her husband. Swider-Peltz thinks their combined approach was just right. "I think it was an ideal way to raise children," she says. "Sometimes you need words of encouragement to fill in the gaps, and sometimes you need to realize you have to work for it."

PRACTICAL HELP

Important as verbal affirmation is, sometimes it's not enough. Good parents supplement their affirming words with practical help, when and if it's needed. Nancy Tecson, for example, now a musician and mother, remembers that while her father encouraged her academic achievement by passing out copies of her impressive report cards to his friends, her mother helped her in a more concrete way. "If I was having trouble in some class or needed to be tested in something, Mom was the one who would do that," she says. "She would show me how to study. While my dad was more of a cheerleader, my mom would help me figure out problems."

Like Nancy Tecson, Grace Ketterman has appreciative memories of the tangible encouragement she got from her parents. In an era when few families had typewriters, Ketterman's mother would lovingly copy her children's school papers for them with her flawless penmanship. As busy and tired as she was with seven children, she would spend hours going over their spelling words, teaching them their flash cards, whatever it took to help them learn. Ketterman's father, an avid reader, taught the children by reading aloud to them or stopping to comment on an idea while he read magazines, books, or papers. "Even though they came from a Pennsylvania Mennonite background, from a strict, enclosed group that didn't generally encourage women in medicine," observes Ketterman, who is now a pediatrician and child psychiatrist, "my parents pushed me to make the most of my life. I think that evidenced a belief in my worth and inculcated a sense of God's plan and power and purpose in my life."

Molly Cline, a scientist and mother, points out that in order to be encouraging, the help that parents give their children should be just that—help. If parents take over their children's projects, it diminishes self-worth instead of enhancing it. "My parents wouldn't do things for me," she says, "but they would always help me. I remember in grade school my mother helped me write an essay entitled 'Blessings from Heaven.' My dad would help me by reviewing speeches and other things I had written. My parents were my first coaches and mentors."

Sometimes the practical help that children need in order to achieve their potential takes the form of opportunities they wouldn't otherwise have or resources they wouldn't otherwise get. Steve Roskam, a physician and father of two, says his father is a good example of a parent who provides encouragement by making opportunities for his children. "My dad opened a lot of doors for me," he says. "For example, I was heavily involved in gymnastics in high school, but my high school wasn't allowing us to train all year round. I was upset by that because I wanted to excel. My dad said, 'Well, do you want to go some place and train for a year?' And I said, 'Uh, sure.' So through his diligent efforts, I ended up with the West German Olympic team. I was a sixteen-year-old kid. I wasn't anywhere near their level, but I was over there training with them for a year because my dad pursued it. He had made cold calls to strangers, saying, 'My son is going to be over there, can he train with you?' And the answer was, 'Well, nobody's ever asked before. Sure.' So I dropped out of high school for a year and trained."

VISUALIZING SUCCESS

Every so often, Benjamin Carson's mom would get in the car and drive both Carson and his brother out to the affluent neighborhoods where she worked as a maid. She would describe to her young sons how her employers lived and then say, 'These people don't spend all night watching television. They're studying. That's why they live here.' Then she'd drive back to their dilapidated neighborhood in Detroit's ghetto. "What do these people do?" she'd say as she drove through streets littered with broken bottles. "Look at them hanging around, drinking, and watching television. That's why they live where they do. You have a choice about which way you want to be."

Seeing that graphic distinction between achievers and

nonachievers, says Carson, now a renowned pediatric neuro-surgeon, made a deep impression on him. That, and finally learning to read in the fifth grade, helped him to visualize success. "All of a sudden I started to see myself differently," Carson observes. "I began to see myself as having all kinds of potential. And once I started visualizing myself as successful and in control of my own destiny, I saw poverty as only a temporary setback. I got that vision from my mother."

CONSISTENT PRESENCE

Good parents encourage their children with their presence. Like Ron Hutchcraft, many grown children of good parents say that some of their warmest memories are of their parents' presence at important events in their lives. "I remember my parents' presence at just about everything that ever mattered to me," Hutchcraft says, "whether it was the Sunday-school Christmas program or the Youth for Christ national Bible quiz championships or the VFW essay contest or the Daughters of the American Revolution spelling bee. Those things might seem small now, but that was my universe then. It seems to me my parents never missed anything."

The events were different in the life of Richard Chase, former president of Wheaton College. But the significance of his parents' presence was the same. Chase competed in a number of rodeos as a kid and thinks he may have won a blue ribbon once or twice. He can't remember for sure because it didn't seem to matter who won. "I just remember it was fun and Dad was there," muses Chase. "Even if we came in last, Dad thought we were the greatest riders in the world. If I was involved in a music program, Mom was there. When I played basketball, even if I only played one minute in the game, I was the star as far as my parents were concerned."

Jon Ebersole, the son of a small-town doctor and his wife, was a little embarrassed as a teenager when his parents showed up at all his athletic events, including some of the practices. A lot of other kids' parents didn't do that. But even so, he says, part of him kind of liked it because he understood the underlying message: "This is important, and we're taking time to do it."

RECOGNITION OF INDIVIDUAL STRENGTHS

Wise parents realize that, to be effective, encouragement should be specific rather than general. While grown children of good parents had a general sense of their parents' approval, they needed—and got—specific feedback that helped them identify their strengths.

As Colorado ranchers, it would have been understandable if Gregg Roeber's parents had encouraged him to pursue the activities considered suitable for ranchers' sons: outdoor activities and athletics. But they recognized that Gregg's gifts were more cerebral and encouraged him accordingly. "One of the striking things about my parents," says Roeber, who ultimately left the family ranch to pursue an academic career and teach at a university, "is that both of them allowed me to do a great deal of reading. I was encouraged to do it, even though there was always more work to be done than anybody could have done. I remember some of the children on nearby ranches were given quite severe work to do at a very early age. That wasn't the case with me. I had chores to do, but my parents encouraged my interest in learning from the time I was quite young."

Recognizing and supporting individual strengths is especially important when one child is unusually gifted. Dick Martens, an attorney, says one of the characteristics he appreciated most about his parents was their ability to value him for who he was, even though he wasn't the obvious star of the family. "I'm the second kid of two," he explains, "and my older sister is a very gifted person, very bright and energetic. She has perfect pitch, picks things up easily, is a good artist and musician. She plays a number of instruments, sings well, and is a math and science whiz. So it would have been difficult for most anybody to have been a second kid and not feel as if he were eclipsed by the talent of the first. But I think my parents were unusually good at acknowledging that we all have our own strengths and weaknesses and that a person's self-worth really isn't tied up with his or her various talents, that a person is still worthwhile even if he can't do x, y, and z as well as somebody else can. My parents were very supportive of whatever I could do as long as I was doing my best. For example, my sister and I both went through the accelerated math course in high school, but she was the whiz kid. When the college placement tests came around, she got a five in calculus. I got a three or something, which was acceptable to get a proficiency at most colleges, but it didn't get me all the credit. But that was fine with my parents. In their eyes, I was a kid who was doing his best. I had worked hard and that was fine for them. They were able to take a kid as they found him. I think that's very important."

David Handley, the pastor of a large Presbyterian church and, by his own description, the sibling of a "superstar," also thinks that kind of acceptance is important. "My parents were very affirming of who I was as an individual," he recalls. "My brother, who is almost two years older than I, was an egghead academic, valedictorian of his class, a straight, perfect kid. I was more the athlete and rebel. Yet my parents always encouraged my strengths. They were very enthusiastic about my brother's accomplishments, but they always found ways to be there for me by showing up at my athletic events or other things in which I excelled. That said to me, 'Hey, this is just as important as what my brother is doing.'"

David Handley and Dick Martens are both intelligent, talented people; they just happened to be following siblings who appeared to be even more intelligent and talented. So their parents' challenge was to value their strengths without comparing them to their spectacularly gifted siblings. Recognizing and supporting individual strengths is even more important when one child doesn't seem to have any gifts—at least in the eyes of the world.

Mary O'Connor's parents had four children in four years: three girls and a boy. They all went to the same school, and they all did well academically—all of them, that is, except O'Connor's brother. "We didn't know it at the time," says O'Connor, "but he was color blind and probably had some dyslexia. We all had the same teachers, so when this boy who didn't do well came along, they gave him some hard times. But my parents really supported him. When he got into high school, they got him into areas that didn't require academic skills. As things turned out, he didn't go to college, but he got a steady job working for the government, and he's done that job for seventeen years."

SUPPORT WITHOUT PRESSURE

The ability to support and encourage a child without exerting undue pressure is another characteristic of good parents. Timothy Johnson, medical editor for ABC News, says his parents had that ability. "I never felt any pressure to succeed, even though my parents certainly encouraged me to achieve," he explains. "I took piano lessons for many years, for example, and while I was somewhat successful at it, I was certainly never a star. That was more than acceptable to them. They never pushed me to achieve beyond what I could. When I did a poor job at a recital, which was not unusual, they never made an issue of it. They felt I had done my best; that's all I could do. Even though I turned out to be a high achiever, I never felt the pressure to be such. Whenever I did something that was a matter of some achievement, they were quick to let me know how proud they were of that. But on the other hand, they never pushed me to do it in the first place. They had a reward system, but not a demand system. Studying, getting good grades, participating in plays and the debate team were all my own choice. My parents were always supportive and encouraging and happy to have me do these things, but I had no sense that I'd be less loved if I didn't do them."

Janet Getz grew up in a family of high achievers. Her father was a highly successful oil executive. Her mother, trained as a social worker, was an energetic volunteer who created a number of innovative service programs in the various foreign countries they lived in while Getz was growing up. Given her parents' achievements, it wouldn't have been surprising if Getz had felt tremendous pressure to achieve on her parents' terms. But she didn't. "My mom is very skilled in watching people and understanding their hearts and motives and knowing how best to encourage and love them so they can grow," Getz says. "From the time I was little, I knew that all of us were very bright. Yet she never focused on that. She focused on who we were as people. I never felt I had to perform for her. I always knew that whatever I did, I would be loved and accepted, especially by her. She was very pleased by the things we did, but because she listened to us, included us, and talked to us, she was a safe person. We could just be ourselves. She just liked us. I wanted to be the wonderful person I knew she believed I was."

UNCONDITIONAL APPROVAL

Janet Getz's parents *liked* her. That sense of their parents' approval is something that almost all grown children of good parents have in common. Whatever their encouragement style, good parents communicate not only love but also approval to their children. Somehow they manage to convey to their kids that, achievements aside, they just plain like and enjoy them.

"The greatest gift my father gave me was the way he enjoyed being with me," says David Handley. "The greatest show in town was his kids. He was a very successful salesperson when his company wanted him to move to Minneapolis to be an executive vice-president in the company. But he turned down the job. I asked him why in the world would he do that? And he said, 'Because I want to spend time with my family.' I've never forgotten that. I remember exactly where I was when he told me. Looking back, it meant a lot."

Mary O'Connor agrees. "I always felt that our parents enjoyed us," she says. "An Amish man once told me that the Amish people believe it's more important to enjoy children than to love them. I've thought about that ever since I heard it. If you enjoy children, they'll feel loved."

Communicating Approval

So how do parents communicate that they like and enjoy their children? Often it's a simple matter of demeanor. Children are very tuned in, for example, to even the most subtle expressions on their parents' faces. When those expressions are positive, kids' spirits soar.

David Heim's father probably wasn't thinking about what his face was communicating to his son when he attended his son's basketball games. But his beaming expression spoke eloquently of his love and approval. "He was as pleased as punch that I played on the basketball team," recalls Heim. "It showed on his face. He would be there at every game, beaming at me. But the approval I felt had nothing to do with how well I played. He just enjoyed basketball and being around me."

Louis McBurney's parents didn't necessarily show up at all his activities, but nonetheless he felt a total sense of acceptance and approval from them. "It was just the twinkle in their eyes," he says, "the delight in their faces when I would achieve something."

As a child psychiatrist, and the daughter of a twinkly-eyed father, Grace Ketterman knows how important it is for children to be able to read approval in their parents' faces. "Our parents' approval helps us know we've succeeded," she explains. "My dad wasn't very verbal with his approval, but with a wink or twinkle of his eye, by some nonverbal gesture, he would let me know he was proud of me. That helped to build a core of healthy self-esteem in me."

Like Grace Ketterman, many grown children of good parents say their parents' approval wasn't necessarily spoken; it was demonstrated. Janet Getz says, "My mother communicated approval by listening and showing and caring and involving me in her life. I knew she liked me because she included me in things she was doing and accepted my attempts and efforts. She let me explore and try things out and believed I would be able to do them. She didn't desert me in the process but was able to step back and let me grow. When I was with my mother, she was mine 100 percent. If I had a story to tell her, she listened and could tell me the story afterward. She could ask questions that were pertinent.

"People talk a lot about poor self-esteem," Getz continues, "but I never had to worry about that because I knew I was loved. And what that did for me was free me to believe that God really loved me."

Avoiding Too Much of a Good Thing

Gretchen Ziegenhals says her parents' encouraging ways were among their greatest strengths. But she sometimes wonders if maybe they gave her too much of a good thing. "I felt such love and encouragement," Ziegenhals says, "even if I failed. I remember the time I didn't make a high-school play that I really wanted a part in, and I went and sobbed on the couch. My mother sat by me and patted my back. But at times I've thought, *Gee, maybe my parents shouldn't have been quite so encouraging*. At times when I've been disappointed, I've wondered if maybe they should have given me a little more realism. As an adult, I'll fail at something and think, 'But I thought my parents said I was really good at that!' So I think parents can affirm kids almost too much. It hasn't been a big problem for me, but I've sensed it at different points."

Author Madeleine L'Engle feels very strongly that parents can affirm kids too much. "Too much encouragement is very crippling, just as crippling as discouragement," she says. "My parents did the best thing: they never overencouraged or discouraged me. They just let me do it. They would let me show my writing to them. They would read it and tell me what was good about it. Not always bad about it, but something good about it. Sometimes the things I wrote were pretty bad, but they always found something good to say."

Finding something good to say about young L'Engle's writing must have taken a real act of the will when she began to write about them—or people like them. "My father died while I was in my last year of high school," says L'Engle. "And while I was in college, I began to write about a man who went with his wife and their adolescent child to the Alps, looking for a place where he could breathe—just as my parents and I had when we moved to Europe when I was twelve. We were trying to find a healthier place for my father, who had been gassed in World War I and had damaged lungs. My writing knows more than I know, and my stories knew a lot more about my parents' marriage than I knew. But my mother was wonderful. Instead of saying, 'Oh, you've hurt me so terribly!' she'd say, 'It's good, dear. You keep on. You keep on writing!'"

L'Engle's parents knew how to encourage their child without paralyzing her with too much encouragement. Dick

Chase's parents, on the other hand, knew how to let their children fail without paralyzing them with discouragement. "I didn't get a lot of negative stuff," says Chase about his upbringing on a California dairy farm. "I remember tipping over a heavily loaded hay truck in the alfalfa fields, for example. The fields were designed with little berms so that the farmers could flood the fields. You had to go over the berms very carefully, because if you went in at too much of an angle, the truck would tip over. But when that happened, I don't remember much punishment. Dad came by from another field, took his truck, and everybody worked hard. Even though I had tipped over the truck, he said nothing to me about it. We got back in the truck and drove it on. If I made a mistake, it just meant a lot of work to correct it. But if I did something right, it seems to me there was an awful lot of praise. So I wasn't afraid to take risks. I wasn't afraid to make mistakes."

Instead of berating him, Chase's parents let natural consequences be his teacher: he learned that if he made a mistake, it took a lot of work to correct it. Good parents likewise know that allowing their children to experience the natural benefits of doing well is preferable to encouraging them with material rewards. Molly Cline observes: "I studied hard and got good results. My parents talked about my accomplishments a lot, but they never rewarded me with money. They might make a special meal or give me a nod at a family dinner, but material rewards weren't used as incentives. And they never made me feel I was competing with anybody except myself."

ENCOURAGING EXPECTATIONS

Sometimes positive expectations alone can be a form of encouragement, a self-fulfilling prophecy. Chicago *Tribune* columnist Joan Beck says neither of her parents gave a great deal of praise. In fact, she says, both she and her sister felt that their achievements were taken for granted. Their parents just assumed they would do well—and they did. "Both of us were valedictorians of our high school class," says Beck, "but my parents never said much about it. They just smiled and nodded as if this was what they expected. They didn't say, 'You've got to come out on top,' or, 'This is great, we'll go buy you a car.' Nothing was said. It was just expected."

DON'T GIVE UP

It's one thing to be encouraging, even quietly encouraging, when your offspring is valedictorian of her class. It's something else entirely when he appears to be wasting his potential and doesn't even care that he's going nowhere. In a situation like that—a situation Fred Barnes's parents found themselves in during his late teens and early twenties—encouragement may mean just not giving up.

"For a number of years, from the time I was about nineteen to about twenty-four, my parents and I weren't real close," says Barnes, now White House correspondent for *The New Republic* and a regular guest on public television's *The McLaughlin Group*. "After college, I worked for a year at a newspaper in South Carolina, and then I came home and started grad school and worked as a part-time checker at a Safeway store. But I hated grad school, so I quit and just kept my job at the Safeway. I wanted to be a beach bum, but my mother kept encouraging me to go back to journalism. She kept saying, 'Go to the *Star*. You ought to go there.' And, as it turned out, I ran into some guy who was a reporter and wound up getting a job there. I've been in journalism ever since."

Despite plenty of evidence that Barnes was never going to make anything of himself, his mother never gave up on him. He didn't appreciate her encouragement at the time, but as one of the country's most respected journalists, he does now.

WHAT IT ALL MEANS

Encouragement means giving your kids verbal affirmation, practical help, and the gift of your presence at important events in their lives. It means recognizing and supporting your children's individual strengths. It means letting your kids know they can please you. As Ben Carson says, "There's something about knowing someone is super-interested in your doing well—someone whom you can please to the ends of the earth by doing well—to motivate you to work hard."

At the same time, encouragement means letting your kids know they don't have to do well to keep your love. It means letting your kids know you like them, that you approve of them, that you're on their side.

Encouragement means giving your kids compliments they know they've earned—often enough to keep them from getting discouraged, but not so often that the compliments lose their value.

Encouragement means expecting your kids to fulfill their potential, but not expecting so much that they're paralyzed by fear or set up for a collision with a less adoring and more realistic world.

Encouragement is one of the most powerful gifts you can give your children. It is a gift that nurtures competence and confidence and optimism. Good parents know how to encourage.

•TWO•

Show and Tell:
Communicate Your Love

Mother would constantly say, "I love you, sweetheart."

Mary Kay Ash

*My dad would always pick me up in his arms when he came home
and kiss me and say, "I missed you. I'm so glad to be home with you
and Mom."*

Jody Hedberg

*Mine wasn't a demonstrative, huggy family, but I never doubted
my parents loved me. They took care of me.*

Jon Ebersole

My parents told me straight out they loved me. A lot.

Brenda Weaver

IT WOULD SEEM obvious that good parents love their children.
Some people even say that the only really important quality a
parent needs is love. But when you get right down to it,
whether or not you have a feeling of love for your kids is
pretty much irrelevant. Children benefit only from the actions

and expressions associated with love, not from the emotion itself. It's a good thing, because feelings waver and wobble, especially when kids go through the often-treacherous teenage years. But you can *communicate* love to your children even when you don't feel it.

Good parents may or may not feel loving toward their children at any given moment, but they consistently express their love to their kids. They express that love in many ways: physical affection, verbal expression, loving actions, sacrifice, availability, pride, respect, tenderness, grace, and forgiveness. Some children receive—and perceive—one form of loving expression more easily than others. But since kids rarely tell their parents which form of love communicates best to them, wise parents try both to show and tell their love with more than one language.

PHYSICAL AFFECTION

Many grown children of good parents say their parents were very physical in their expression of love. David Handley's memories are typical: "My parents were affectionate," he recalls. "I always felt a lot of warmth from my mother, lots of cuddling and embracing. And I remember getting into bed with my father when I was maybe seven or eight, and he would read his J. B. Phillips translation of the Bible with me. That was a very warm feeling."

Interestingly, a number of the grown children I spoke with said their fathers were more outwardly affectionate than the cultural norm. "My father was a very touchy person," Dick Martens observes. "I think most men are relatively uncomfortable with touching. Our society feels discomfort with men touching other men. But as a child and to this day, my father and I embrace and kiss. He's probably the only man that I would ever kiss on the cheek, but when I see him, that's what we do."

O'Ann Steere says that, coming from a very warm, affectionate family, she didn't realize that her father was unusually affectionate until she got to college. "I remember in my sociology class the professor asked, 'What age were you when your father stopped kissing you?'" she says. "I thought *My father has never stopped kissing me.* I was a senior in college before I realized my peers' fathers had stopped kissing them when they were early teenagers."

VERBAL EXPRESSION

Loving words are tremendously powerful. Children remember them long after they're expressed. But good parents know that loving words need to be repeated. As Molly Cline says, "We would always say we loved each other. Every day."

O'Ann Steere's family had a wonderful secret expression that came out of a joke. "My dad called down on the intercom one night," she explains, "and said, 'Don't forget.' I said, 'Don't forget what?' And he'd forgotten! So he said, 'Uh . . . don't forget I love you.' So after that, we'd holler out, 'Don't forget.' One year, my dad ordered for us T-shirts that said 'Don't forget.' And when my dad kissed me good-bye at my wedding, the last thing he said was, 'Don't forget.'"

Public Expressions of Love

Good parents express their love publicly as well as privately. Janet Getz says she'll never forget that when her dad retired, the things he talked about weren't all the successes, the marvelous things he'd done as head of Amoco Europe and Amoco Egypt, but about his family. "He talked about each one of us," she recalls, "what we were doing and how much he cared for us. I really felt valued and loved. And I remember one time when my mom called me on the phone and said she'd been to a retreat where they were asked who was 'gospel woman'—someone who reflected the gospel—for them. And she said, 'When I was asked, I thought of you. You were the person for me.' I thought, *Oh my gosh, for me, she is too. So I knew my parents valued and loved me.*"

LOVING ACTIONS

A surprising number of interviewees said their parents rarely if ever expressed their love through physical affection or even by saying, "I love you." But even so, they never doubted their parents' affection and commitment. For these families, actions truly spoke louder than words.

Take neurosurgeon Doug Anderson's family, for example. Even though his mom isn't a "touchy-feely type" person, Anderson always knew she loved him. "When I was a little kid," he says, "I would get poison ivy for two or three weeks out of every summer. I'd have poison ivy on every part of my body. I could barely sit. And my mother would take care of me so, so meticulously. I later learned that half of her therapies did more harm than good," he laughs, "but I never doubted how much she loved me. I'll never forget that. And I knew that if I got sick, I could go to my mom, and she'd take care of me. Even when I was a resident in neurosurgery—I wasn't married yet and I was on call on Christmas day—and I got sick. When you get sick on Christmas, you can't call somebody and say, 'Can you cover for me? I'm sick.' So I just went in. I was deathly ill and afterward I remember wrapping myself in a hospital blanket, walking to my car, and driving to my mom's. I wanted Mom to take care of me. That's probably the easiest way to explain how easy it was to know she loved me. I was so cared for."

Lowell Olberg can't remember his parents ever saying, "I love you," but neither can he remember ever feeling any question about it. Why else would his father give up a big promotion? "He was offered a job as a salesman," Olberg, now a successful salesman himself, recalls, "but it meant being away from the family. He didn't want to do that, so he stayed in the factory." That decision communicated love to his children in a powerful way.

Mary O'Connor says her mother wasn't one to gush it up, to hug and kiss her kids all the time, but she wouldn't hesitate to drive five hours to have lunch with Mary or one of her siblings. Likewise, her father is very much a doer, not a talker. "He likes to fix things for us, build things for us, take us somewhere," O'Connor says.

SACRIFICE

Benjamin Carson probably never would have become the renowned pediatric neurosurgeon he is today were it not for his mother's sacrifices. With her third-grade education and failed marriage to a man she discovered was a bigamist, Sonya Carson had few prospects for success in life. But she was determined to improve the prospects for her sons, to give them a chance to get out of the cycle of poverty and failure that seemed to hover over their ghetto neighborhood like a radioactive cloud. So she worked as a maid to support her kids and help them fulfill what she firmly believed was their unlimited potential.

"She raised two sons on her own with no resources," says Carson. "We knew that everything she did was for us. My mother was a very attractive woman, and she had no end of suitors who would have done anything for her. But she basically brushed them off and went out and worked two and three jobs to give us a head start in life.

"She'd pretty much given up on herself," he continues, "but we understood she was sacrificing for us."

Carson and his brother saw and heard the message in their mother's sacrifice: she loved them. Other grown children of good parents say they also perceived love in acts of sacrifice. It should be pointed out, of course, that children don't respect parents who make themselves into doormats. Martyrdom is rarely healthy when it comes to family life. But the memories of grown children of good parents are strong evidence that strategic sacrifices, made in love, can have a powerful impact.

Mary Kay Ash remembers how she desperately wanted a typewriter, which her mother couldn't afford. Ash recalls, "She somehow saved the money and bought me a Woodstock typewriter, which would be like buying a kid a computer today. It was a big investment." The conclusion young Ash drew from this act of sacrifice? "It was pretty obvious my parents loved me."

Radio talk-show co-host Melinda Schmidt can't remember ever hearing her parents tell her they loved her, at least not in words. But, she says, their sacrifices spoke of love in a very clear way. "They were very giving in a gracious, loving way," she says. "They'd do a lot of special things for us. Not spoiling things, but a lot of surprise things. Like letting me go to Florida on a trip with a girlfriend. Or saving a lot of money so I could go do something I really wanted to do. I knew it cost them a great deal to give me those opportunities. They also sent me to a Christian grade school when they had nothing. That to me was a real example of love."

AVAILABILITY

Social worker Jon Ebersole reflected on how his parents communicated their love. "Dad would show his love with his time. I don't think there's a more powerful way to say it, to really get the message across. Especially to kids."

Good parents know, as Jon Ebersole's father knew, that children often equate love with availability. So they communicate their love with the gifts of time and attention, gifts that, as Timothy Johnson points out, can mean more than words. "My parents would make sure verbally that we knew they loved us," he recalls. "But as I look back with more insight, I'd say they demonstrated love most of the time through everyday care and presence. My father loved to organize family outings and trips. He made it clear that was something he really liked to do for his boys. And my mother just provided all those things you take for granted as kids and don't appreciate until you look back on it."

Good parents make themselves available to their kids even when it's not convenient. Molly Cline recalls, "They were always there for us, regardless of their personal mood or circumstances. They never said, 'I'm tired. I can't talk to you now,' or, 'I don't feel like it.' I think that's phenomenal."

Gerry Koenig has similar memories: "I recall my father hitting ground balls to us or fly balls to us after a long day of work and even when he wasn't feeling so well," he says. "I had a clear sense that I was worth something to him. I was not a bother."

Often, emotional availability is as important, or more important, than mere physical presence. Dick Martens observes, "I always had the feeling my parents would be there. They were extremely loyal, and that was comforting. They were willing to listen to hear what I had to say and not necessarily to give the quick response, the platitude. They kind of let the situation be there, to let me know they were there if I needed them, without necessarily saying, 'Well, you should do this or that or the other thing.'"

PRIDE, RESPECT, AND TENDERNESS

Children have their antennae tuned to the wavelength of love. They pick it up in their parents' expressions of pride, respect, and tenderness. Even the look on a parent's face can speak of love. "The Bible verse, 'I will guide you with mine eye,' is extremely meaningful to me," says Grace Ketterman. "I knew that from my father. He was not at all huggy, but he indicated his love by the look in his eye. Affection, tenderness—that was so beautifully expressed from his eyes."

David Handley can't put his finger on what it was exactly, but something about his parents' expressions communicated their great pride in him. "I remember an intense pride," he says. "'This is my kid.' That kind of thing. There was a sense of, 'You've really got what it takes.'" Because his parents obviously thought so well of him, Handley was able to think well of himself; he developed a healthy core of self-esteem. And it didn't hurt that his parents valued his thoughts and opinions. "I remember my mother investing my opinions with respect," he recalls. "She seemed to be real curious about what I was thinking. She'd say, 'What do you think about this?' and she seemed to be genuinely interested."

Parents who consider their children's feelings and opinions when making decisions that affect the whole family are not only investing their kids in the outcome but also communicating love in the process. "One thing that impressed me," says Jay Kesler, "was that when my parents would buy a car, they would take us and let us look at it and tell them what we thought. We felt important. Once they wanted to move, and we went to look at another house. I even remember the name of the street. Victoria Street. I was about six, and my sister was eight. We all went and looked at it and talked about moving into a nicer, bigger house and going to a different school. But we didn't want to leave our school. And we didn't move. We all thought our opinions affected that."

It's not always feasible to include children in decision making, or in all levels of decision making, but good parents let their children have a say whenever possible. It might not be appropriate to let children decide whether or not to redecorate the living room, for example, but once the decision to do it is made, it can be a wonderful message of love to include the kids in the plans. Mary O'Connor recalls, "Whenever we had a decision to make about how we were going to decorate a room or something, my father would always say, 'Now what do you kids think?' We always got to be part of that. If we said pink, it would be pink. 'Where should we go on vacation?' We always got to be part of the planning."

GRACE

Good parents understand—and strategically implement—the principle of grace. Theologians define grace as "unmerited favor." Kids call it giving them a break. The principle of grace points up an apparent irony, a creative tension, in child-rearing: it's important to be consistent in administering discipline. It's crucial to help kids understand the consequences of their actions. But a little unmerited favor, a little grace, can be a powerful thing.

What convinced me of the power of parental grace was not only the number of grace stories my interviewees had to tell but also the vividness with which they remembered them. Writer Nancy Gruben, for example, tells of a very happy childhood memory, an experience she refers to as an example of "hope lost and hope restored." "We were driving home from church," she recalls, "and I was waving my Sunday-school paper out the window. My dad said, 'Don't wave that; it will blow away.' I kept doing it, and eventually it blew out the window. I, of course, screamed and cried. My brother said, 'We told you not to do it.' But my father stopped the car and went into the field and looked and found it and gave it to me. I knew I had done the wrong thing, and I lost the paper because of it. But instead of my father saying, 'This action has consequences, now you live with it,' he stopped the car and found the paper. I've never forgotten that he did that for me."

Grace Ketterman has her own story of hope lost and restored. "In the early days of synthetic fabrics, I remember having a beautiful satin petticoat," she says. "In those days, we had to iron everything, and I was in the process of ironing the petticoat when I let the iron get too hot. I set it down, but when I lifted it up, long strings of melted fabric went from the iron to the ironing board. My father was going through the kitchen at the time, and I expected a scolding about my carelessness. But instead he got this wonderful twinkle in his eye and made a swooping gesture with his hands, as if the strings were swooping. For days afterward, he would make that funny gesture. It was a secret between the two of us. Instead of making that a horror—we knew such poverty—it was one of those things that brought forgiveness and hope and remedy in a tight situation."

Grace Disguised as a Pony

Parental grace can take many forms. When Elaine Kirk was a young girl, grace came disguised as a pony. One memorable day, a man stopped by her parents' farm to look at a pony— her pony—with the thought of buying it. That pony was her life, and she didn't want her father to sell it. So when the would-be buyer asked her father to have Elaine ride the pony so he could see how it acted, she got on the pony and took off. "They didn't see me again," admits Kirk ruefully. "I feared a little bit coming back home later in the day—I was afraid of what my dad might say—but he just chuckled and said, 'Well, I guess you're going to keep your pony.' He didn't chastise me a bit for taking off, even though I left them high and dry."

Parents who never hold their children responsible for their actions, of course, run the risk of producing some very undesirable character traits in their children. But parents who have done their job and know their children are basically responsible—and are genuinely sorry for mistakes or misbehavior—are free to extend the gift of grace when it seems appropriate. Gerry Koenig will never forget the gift of grace his mother gave him as a child. "One time my parents went into town to do the weekly grocery shopping and left the children at home," he explains. "While they were gone, my sister and I got into a squabble, and she chased me around the table with a broom. She swung and I ducked and she knocked a plaque off the wall. It broke into a thousand pieces. So we glued it back together, doing a very careful job. We put it back on the wall and didn't tell our parents. Well, several months later, my mother was doing the spring cleaning and she observed this. And she said, 'How did this happen?' The interesting thing is, when we finally confessed our wrong, she didn't overreact. Instead of saying, 'Oh, my treasured piece!' she said, 'Well, you probably had to live with that for a while, so you probably learned your lesson.' She handled it that way instead of trying to get an extra pound of flesh. That was significant."

Nancy Gruben's father would have been justified in letting her experience the consequences of her behavior, since she ignored his advice. It would have been understandable if Grace Ketterman's dad had reproved her for carelessness given their tight financial circumstances. Elaine Kirk's father and Gerald Koenig's mother would have been within their rights if they had come down hard on their kids for their behavior. But they chose to exercise grace—and their kids have never forgotten it.

FORGIVENESS

Forgiveness is another spiritual principle that applies to parenting. Because God loves us, he offers us forgiveness. Because parents love their children, they offer them forgiveness. And in forgiving, they communicate their love.

Forgiving your kids doesn't mean you don't let them know when they've done something wrong. And it doesn't mean children don't get put 'in the doghouse' from time to time. It does mean that reproof and recriminations are short-lived, that kids know they're not in danger of losing their parents' love because they messed up. Dick Martens reflects, "My parents certainly let me know when I was on the outs. But I was on the outs only for a relatively short period of time, which I think is good. It's been a plus in my life, and it's been a plus in my own family. When a grievance occurs, we openly address it, and then it's over. If I messed up, my parents let me know it, but then they forgave me, and we all went on."

Loving Enough to Forgive

Even the best parents sometimes have trouble loving enough to forgive. Joan Petersen's parents had to struggle to forgive Joan's adopted sister, Marcy, when she became pregnant out of wedlock at age seventeen. As a black child adopted by a white family, Marcy had struggled to find herself throughout a stormy and rebellious adolescence that caused her parents a lot of pain. When she got pregnant, her parents were not only shocked but also hurt and humiliated. "My parents took it very personally," says Petersen. "They felt they had failed as parents. My dad was ashamed to go to church. But over the nine months of Marcy's pregnancy, they were able to work through a lot of frustration and anger. And in the end, it brought Marcy and my parents closer together. Marcy gave birth to a healthy baby boy and named him after our brother who died. My parents are just in love with him, and they're now in the early stages of helping Marcy work on a plan for the future—finding a job, taking care of the baby, being able to support a child on her own."

Joan Petersen knew her parents loved her because they told her so. Because they spent time with her. Because they did special things for her. Her parents did all those things with Marcy too. But Marcy didn't fully perceive their love until they were able to forgive her.

"I'm really impressed that my parents were able to forgive," reflects Petersen. "They didn't compromise on where they stood. They told Marcy, 'We really don't think this is God's plan. But we love you and will love this baby. We'll support you through this.' That was really exciting. You could really see that love was there. Not just love when you're good and you do things right. It was there even when you messed up."

The all-you-need-is-love philosophy is a fallacy when it comes to raising kids. Kids need a lot more, as the next chapters will attempt to show. But make no mistake: parents who give their kids everything else—discipline, encouragement, safety, spiritual values, all the rest—but fail to communicate love, have failed their children in a significant way.

Express your love physically, verbally, and through your actions. Be willing to make strategic sacrifices. Make yourself available. Give your kids the gifts of pride and respect and tenderness. Be sensitive to when your kids need a little grace and forgiveness.

Children have amazing antennae for love. But it's your responsibility to communicate it.

· THREE ·

Create a Positive Atmosphere

My mother had a radiant good cheer. I think that's very helpful to a child growing up—looking at life in a positive way.

Timothy Johnson

I've seen some families where they're very polite with each other, but they can't laugh and lighten up. In my family, life wasn't so serious. We could laugh at each other.

Melinda Schmidt

My mother always said, "You can do what you want to do as long as you stick to it and do your best. God has given you a talent. It's your responsibility to try to bring that potential to its ultimate."

Nancy Swider-Peltz

LUIS PALAU REMEMBERS his mother singing all the time. Dick Chase recalls his father clowning at the piano and teasing his friends in a good-natured way. Gretchen Ziegenhals remembers her parents' ability to see the silver lining in every cloud. Janice Rohne Long pictures her parents as always laughing

43

and smiling. David Heim can't forget his father's unsinkable enthusiasm.

Like other good parents, these fathers and mothers created a positive atmosphere in their homes. They exuded humor. They faced painful experiences with joy. They communicated hope. They exhibited a "can-do" attitude. They had a sense of adventure about life. They chose to take a positive view of other people. And when they opened their mouths, they spoke words of blessing.

APPROACHING LIFE WITH HUMOR

Radio speaker Ron Hutchcraft says he's found a sense of humor to be a great gift in the ministry. Not only is it an entree to relationships, he says, but a great way to salt the truth. It's also, he believes, a saving grace in families. Hutchcraft's parents were gifted with unsinkable humor.

"My dad was basically the one with the sense of humor," he recalls with a chuckle. "My mom had to take it—that was her sense of humor. My dad was a big tease, and she got picked on constantly. Somewhere along the way, I started chiming in with my dad. We became an aggravating duo. I can remember, for example, that my mom learned to drive a little later in life, and we'd take our car out by the Lake Calumet region near the Indiana-Illinois border while she practiced. My dad was just teasing her constantly, talking to her about how she was hitting the brakes, and I'd sit in the back seat doing this overly dramatic swan dive. I'd hit the floor with a thud whenever she hit the brakes. That was probably the point when I thought my dad's humor was something I wanted to copy, that I wanted to handle life with humor."

The ability to handle life with humor seems to be a key ingredient of good parenting. But, as Dick Chase points out, parenting with humor doesn't mean you have to be a stand-up comedian. "I don't remember jokes particularly," says

Chase, "but we always had a lot of laughter in our house. Mom was a piano teacher, and Dad played the piano by ear. He would make up these funny, crazy songs with grotesque chords, and Mom used to needle him and laugh and try to show him what to do. But he'd just bend down and bang away. He'd tease people an awful lot when they'd come in the home. He'd even tease our dates."

Throwing Dignity to the Wind

Good parents have enough of a sense of humor to give up their dignity once in a while. Dick Marten recalls, "My father was a person who could be kidded. Every once in a while he'd hoist us on his shoulders and run around. He was thirty-nine when I was born, so he was no kid. But we had a lot of good laughs. When we'd play cards, for example, sometimes we'd just really have a belly laugh. He had a sense of ease and comfort."

Melinda Schmidt has similar memories. "If someone was doing something ridiculous—if Mom was doing some crazy cooking thing—we could laugh and tease about it and it was all very good-humored," she says. "We just had a lighthearted way of looking at things."

It's that lighthearted way of looking at life as a whole that seems to make such an impact on children, that gives them hope and confidence even when the chips are down. Timothy Johnson reflects, "My mother especially had a sense of humor about the way she dealt with everyday life. She was quick to laugh about life circumstances, whether good or bad. She was a positive, radiant person who gave me a positive outlook on life, because that attitude rubs off on a child." A positive outlook also rubs off on spouses—as evidenced by the fact that Johnson's father would often join his wife in laughing at their sons' childhood hijinks. "I can remember that when my brother and I would do typical sibling stuff—get in fights and damage our clothes or break things around the house—my parents would sometimes talk about it and start laughing," recalls Johnson. "While they would make it clear they didn't approve and certainly didn't encourage it, when those things would come up in family gatherings, they would tend to chuckle about it."

Gentle Humor

While a sense of humor seems to be characteristic of healthy families—and good parents—not just any kind of humor will do. Only gentle humor, administered with a light touch, seems to be perceived positively by children. Like Mary O'Connor and David Heim, most grown children of good parents say their parents' humor was never sarcastic or biting. "My parents had a sense of humor, but it was never hurtful," says O'Connor. "Their humor was very dry. For example, sometimes we'd go into our bedroom and my father would have gone in before us and taken all our stuffed animals and arranged them on their heads or something."

David Heim, now managing editor of *The Christian Century,* agrees that parental humor is positive only when it is without barbs. "One thing that stands out about my parents is that sarcasm was never their form of humor," he says. "My dad, for example, really enjoyed good stories, especially stories about the church. But they were always told with a good heart. Negative humor was never a part of my growing up."

Injecting Hope through Humor

Like Mary Poppins, who knew that "a spoonful of sugar makes the med'cine go down," wise parents use a touch of humor to take the sting out of a potentially unpleasant situation. Child psychiatrist Grace Ketterman observes, "Humor balances out the seriousness in life. It's part of the hopefulness in life, part of the positive side. It makes us take things a little less seriously. It implies balance."

Ketterman's father knew this intuitively, even without the benefit of higher education. "I remember meeting my dad at the bottom of the stairs from where he called me," recalls Ketterman. "I could see a twinkle in his eye. He took me by the shoulders, walked me to the place where I was supposed to have filled the wood box and just pointed to it and to the back door. I knew perfectly well I had forgotten to do that. His few words and slight tinge of humor were an absolutely marvelous emotional approach to the situation."

Using Humor to Ease Life's Transitions
Good parents know how to use humor to teach their children or ease them through a life transition or gently make a point, as Gerald Koenig's father did. Take the way he informed his son that he was getting a little too big for an Easter nest. At Easter time, Koenig and his siblings used bricks and stones and straw to make nests, into which their parents would put their Easter eggs, chocolates, and other treats. "When my parents felt you were old enough that you really shouldn't build this nest anymore, my father would come up with these unusual ways of indicating to you that you had outgrown the tradition," recalls Koenig. "When I reached a certain age, he picked up some dried road apples, put a wire in them, dipped them in a bucket of paint and put them in my nest. I came around the house and thought, *Ah, I've still got something in my nest*—until I got close and realized they weren't Easter eggs! It was a humorous way of getting across a message."

Seeing Humor in Difficult Times
Effective parents also use humor to get through difficult circumstances. In so doing, they teach their children that

nothing is so consequential that it can't be overcome. "One of the clearest things I remember about my dad," says O'Ann Steere, "was when he bought this jewelry business and we moved to Illinois. He had planned on retiring, but when he heard about this business he thought, *How am I going to tell God I retired at age forty-six?* So the plan was to work for ten years and give everything he made to missions. But the day he bought the business, it burned down. I remember we drove down to spend the evening with him, and I thought, *Does God think this is funny?* But my dad said, 'I guess God can live without my donations.'

"The next day we were carrying things out of the soot, and my dad was carrying this grandfather clock. This woman came rushing out to see if he was injured, and he said, 'I guess I should just buy a wristwatch like everybody else.' In light of the fact that his business had just burned down, I think that kind of humor is amazing. He just figured you could laugh or cry, and you might as well laugh."

JOY DESPITE PAIN

Not all good parents crack jokes in the face of life's difficulties. But some of the best parents seem to be able to stay positive even when their lives appear to be crumbling around them. Judy Anderson was studying at North Park College when she got the news that her mother, a missionary in Africa, would be undergoing a radical mastectomy at a mission hospital in Zaire. Confronted with the possibility that her mother might die, Judy felt as if her world were falling apart. But her mother faced her uncertain future with a sense of hope and trust, just as Judy's dad had handled his near death from bleeding ulcers four years earlier.

"My parents always saw the positives," explains Anderson, "even when things were difficult. They always felt, 'How can we be so lucky? We are the most blessed people in the world.'

They knew that all things work together for those who trust. And they trusted. They had joy. They always had joy. That rubbed off on us."

The gifts Judy Anderson received from her parents—the ability to see the positive, the sense of trust, the joy, the flexibility, and the humor—still carry her through crises in her own family. Several years ago, Anderson's son Chad was diagnosed with a brain tumor. Although some of the world's most renowned pediatric neurosurgeons performed surgery to remove the tumor, they weren't able to get it all out. Chad came home on a monitor—itself both a gift and a curse—and the Andersons began a cruel roller-coaster ride of sleepless nights, moments of hope, and hours of despair. Today, seventeen-year-old Chad's future remains uncertain. Anderson and her husband, Dick, have experienced the full range of emotions that any loving parent would feel when faced with the possible death of a much-loved child. But through it all, Anderson has never lost her ability to trust, to see the positive, to celebrate. And for that, she credits her parents.

"Look at my life," Anderson says. "I should be a wreck. I should be a neurotic falling apart. But I'm not because I have seen my parents survive crises. I exercise; I have a strong, supportive network of friends; and I eat well. My parents modeled that response for me. God gave them the ability to look at things from the positive angle, to make opportunities out of challenges. Those are all important. We also see life as a gift from God, a gift that can't be assumed as indefinite. We try to make the most of each day."

Keep On Keeping On

Good parents teach their children—by word and by example—that even when it's not possible to smile in the face of tragic circumstances, it's important to push through them, to keep going, to persevere.

When Jon Ebersole was a child, his parents always seemed happy and content. In fact, he always thought that was the full picture of his parents until he reached his early twenties. Then, he says, he looked back and saw the realities of their lives. "I realized they were sometimes sad and angry and hurt, but they didn't talk about it much," he reflects. "In some ways that's probably not good. But the good part of it was, they just kept going. Their approach was, whatever comes, you deal with it and go on. You don't get sidetracked lamenting something. You just do it. That's a very necessary part of life, to keep going, no matter what happens. Looking back, I'm glad I have that solid foundation."

Kathy Beito, who works for a mission organization, says she knows a lot of people consider the stoicism so characteristic of her upbringing in a Norwegian-American family to be a bit unhealthy. But she remains unconvinced because it has helped her get through some very difficult life circumstances. Like the death of two of her childhood friends. "I remember my parents explaining that was part of life and its hurts now but I'd be okay," Beito recalls. "That's part of the culture I grew up in in northern Minnesota. Maybe some people would consider it a weakness, but I've lived it and I know that what my parents said is true. You have to push through no matter how hard it seems at the time. You'll get through."

Luis Palau's parents could have thrown up their hands—or huddled hopelessly together—in the face of their neighbors' frequent derision about their evangelical Protestant Christianity. But instead of developing a siege mentality, Palau's family cheerfully shared their faith with anyone and everyone with whom they came in contact. Almost every weekend, they would climb on trucks with other Protestant families and travel to nearby towns, evangelizing the whole way.

"We'd be singing, throwing Bible tracts to people on the side of the road, having a lot of fun," Palau recalls. "Even though we were part of a despised minority, we had a happy home."

Gretchen Ziegenhals says her parents not only lived out a positive approach to life—like the time her father uncomplainingly gave up a much-needed summer vacation to go help his dying mother wrap up housekeeping so she could come live with them—but they also very intentionally helped her find a positive angle to what seemed to her at the time to be tragedies.

"As I look back on the major disappointments in my life," Ziegenhals says, "I realize my parents were really good about helping me see the silver lining. I remember right after I graduated from high school, right when I was getting ready to go off to college, I got mononucleosis. It was terrible. I had a terrible case and had to defer my admission to college because I had to stay in bed for about five or six months. Here I was, all packed with all my little argyle socks and sweaters, and my dad sat down with me and said, 'Look, you can just mope for a year or you can turn this into something really useful. I want you to take a paper and pencil and list the pros and cons of having to stay home.' And he made me come up with goals for myself, including goals I could do in bed. So I came up with some: stop biting my nails; pick one author I had enjoyed in high school and start reading up; get a jump on the German I wanted to study in college, things like that. And he helped flesh out some of these things. My parents just had a very positive approach."

AN ATMOSPHERE OF HOPE

One of the characteristics of people who suffer from depression, psychiatrists say, is a sense of helplessness and hopelessness about the future. Depressed people feel they are powerless in the face of circumstances, that nothing they do can effect a change in their lives. Often, experts say, this sense of helplessness is learned.

Good parents teach their children they are not helpless. They exude confidence and competence themselves—and their infectious can-do attitude transmits itself to their kids. No parent has transmitted this attitude more successfully than Benjamin Carson's mother, who found herself having to raise two young sons on her own with only a third-grade education. Sonya Carson never adopted a victim's mentality. She never threw up her hands and said, "All these things are against me." Instead, she said, "There is a way. There is a way I can do something for myself with my God-given talent." That can-do attitude permeated the atmosphere in the Carson home. Benjamin Carson recalls, "We had a saying in our house: 'Mr. I can't died.' We were never supposed to say, 'I can't do' something." The local school system said the Carson boys weren't college material, but Mrs. Carson said they were. She believed they could make it in college, and they did. The entire weight of American history and the realities of Benjamin Carson's life as a poor black child growing up in a ghetto stood as compelling evidence that he was an unlikely candidate to become a doctor. But, thanks in large part to his mother's confidence in him, to the positive kind of determination she passed on to him, Carson became not just a doctor, but a world-renowned pediatric neurosurgeon.

When Mary O'Connor's little brother developed what appeared to be a life-threatening case of spinal meningitis, her parents faced the prospect of his death with the same steadfastness that they exhibited every day of their lives. "It was terrible," observes O'Connor, "but my parents didn't crumble. We just prayed together." The little boy recovered, but even if he hadn't, O'Connor believes her parents would have been able to cope despite their pain. "I always had the feeling that, no matter what happened, Mom could get us through it," she says. "My parents imparted a sense of, 'No matter what happens to you, you can make it. No matter what the problem you're facing, it's worth working through.' I think I learned that by just seeing it in their own lives. I never saw them get flapped by anything. And they didn't really come from easy circumstances. But, no matter what the problem was, I never had the feeling they couldn't handle it."

SEEING BEYOND THE LIMITS

Good parents don't seem to see the limitations that other people see, and consequently their children don't either. Take David Heim's parents, for example. His father was a minister; his mother was a teacher. They didn't have much money, but they gave David a sense that anything worth doing could be done, regardless of the costs involved.

"It strikes me that whenever we kids asked to do something, it was always discussed in terms of whether it was a good thing to do, never in terms of money," Heim recalls. "It never occurred to me, for example, that I couldn't go to any college I wanted to or that money would be a factor. Of course it was. But my parents always gave me the sense that it would work out if it was an important thing to do. I don't even remember a serious conversation about whether or not we could afford the private college I wanted to go to. It was just assumed we would find a way to do it. I do remember my dad saying in a pleased manner, 'Well, I sent off a check today, and I think we're going to be able to do it.' But in my mind, it was never an issue. I never had a sense that their agenda was other than, 'What's good and important for you to do?'"

Molly Cline has similar memories of her parents: "I never had a brand new bicycle in my life, but we could have been the richest or poorest family in town, and it wouldn't have been reflected in my parents' attitude. They never had a poor-me attitude. They were always content with what they had.

Money was not a limiting factor in enjoying life. I remember once I got some shoes on sale at a shoe store that I guess was considered a classy store. One of my classmates said, 'Boy, it must be nice to shop at a store like that.' My mother and I laughed about that because we probably waited until the shoes went on sale and only splurged that one season. My mom says sometimes we didn't have two extra nickels to rub together. But we had every kind of lesson you could imagine. Our home, our clothing was nice. My mother didn't have ten outfits, but she always looked good. She acted beautiful, and she was."

AN ADVENTUROUS ATTITUDE

Janet Getz spent much of her childhood moving from state to state and country to country. Her family moved every time her oil executive father was transferred, which was often. Some children would be bitter about such a vagabond existence, but Janet isn't and wasn't. "Because of my parents' perspective," she says, "those were wonderful, rich experiences. My parents were excited and enthusiastic about learning about various cultures and how people interacted with one another. So we inherited that from them. It was a great adventure."

A great adventure. That's how good parents seem to view life, and that's how they teach their children to view life. Madeleine L'Engle's parents are a good example. L'Engle loves to recount stories about their spirited approach to life, like the time they sailed to Wales on a whim—a story that comes to mind whenever she glances up at an etching on the wall of her living room, an etching of Castle Conway in Wales. One hot summer night, long before Madeleine was born, when ocean liners plied the seas on a regular basis, L'Engle's mother said, "Oh, Charles, it's so hot. I wish I could go to Castle Conway." L'Engle says, "My father took her hand and said, 'Come on. Out the door. Down to the docks and on to the ship!' No toothbrush. No nothing. Off they went."

SEEING THE GOOD

David Heim says one of his father's most remarkable characteristics was his tendency to see the good in other people. Even though his job as a pastor gave him a vantage point from which to see people's mistakes and character flaws, he chose to focus on their strengths and achievements. That seems to be the case with many good parents.

Timothy Johnson recounts similar experiences: "My mother always had a positive view of other people. I can't remember her saying a bad word about anybody. Even when she would observe something that wasn't ideal, she would always look for a positive side of that person. She'd always have a reason to explain what they did without condemning them. I think my mother didn't have an enemy in the world because she always looked for the best in people and was able to ignore or explain the worst in them."

SAYING THE GOOD

Good parents know that words are powerful—that positive words can bless, that negative words can blight. So they choose to bless with their speech.

Radio pastor Donald Cole lived with a father who had been a Marine drill instructor early in his adult life and who undoubtedly knew how to bellow out commands when the occasion required it. But Cole can't remember a single instance in which his father raised his voice to him. An imposing man who was capable of whipping Marine recruits into shape and shooting the throat out of a bank robber, the elder Cole was nonetheless extremely soft-spoken with his children. What's more, says Cole, both his parents avoided any form of negative communication with their children. "My parents didn't nag at us," he observes. "They didn't chew at us. They created an atmosphere of harmony. I never in my life experienced the yelling I often see in the supermarket. I'll see some people snarling at their kids and yanking them around as if they were toys on a string. These are the people who create criminals. My parents knew you don't have to yell at a kid to make him behave."

David Heim's parents knew that it isn't often helpful for children to listen to critical analyses of people and their personal problems, especially in the church. "One of the remarkable things about my having grown up in a minister's family," says Heim, "was the fact that I never heard any shoptalk about the church. My kids hear a lot more shoptalk about our church's personalities and problems than I did. I'm sure it wasn't because the church didn't have problems and personalities. It was just my dad's attitude toward the church. He felt it was such a privilege to be a minister."

Good parents don't necessarily have easier lives than anyone else, but whatever their life circumstances, they create a noticeably positive atmosphere within their families. They approach life with humor. They maintain hope in the face of difficulties. They keep on going despite inevitable disappointment and adversity. They exude a can-do attitude and a spirit of adventure. They see beyond limits that might thwart others. They bless their children with good words. Good parents live out the admonition of the writer of Philippians, who wrote from a Roman prison cell: "Whatever is true, whatever is noble, whatever is right, whatever is pure, whatever is lovely, whatever is admirable—if anything is excellent or praiseworthy—think about such things. . . . I have learned the secret of being content in any and every situation, whether well fed or hungry, whether living in plenty or in want."

Some good parents live in plenty. Some live in want. Whatever their circumstances, they strive to be content, to stay positive—and in so doing, they give their children a great gift.

◆ FOUR ◆

Nurture Spiritual Values

I wasn't made to be a particular kind of Christian. I was the way I was because of the way my parents lived their lives. It was expected, not forced, that I be honorable, truthful, and love God.

Madeleine L'Engle

We always went to church and Sunday school and young-people's church groups. It was just expected. It wasn't a preachy sort of thing at all. It wasn't onerous, just a natural part of life—what you did.

Joan Beck

The church was the center of our lives as a family. We never missed a service. But I never, ever felt I was forced into Christianity. My parents just enjoyed their faith, and that rubbed off on me.

Luis Palau

GERALD KOENIG IS a grade-school principal. He's been working in the field of education for many years and has had a chance to observe all kinds of children: happy kids and unhappy kids; high achievers and under-achievers; children who show every sign of being on their way to satisfying, productive lives and those who seem destined to graduate from the school of hard knocks.

After rubbing shoulders with kids and their parents for so many years, he's had a chance to develop some theories about what parental actions really make a difference. And he believes that providing a strong religious base is one of the most important things parents can do for their children. He believes that not only because of his observations of hundreds of school children over the years but because that's what his parents did for him.

It's also what most of the adult children interviewed for this book say their parents did for them. Good parents understand that life is more than academic achievement or career success or even a happy family life. Good parents have a strong sense of the transcendent, and one way or another, they convey it to their children.

One of the most fundamental ways good parents transmit spiritual values to their children is by putting them in environments that not only teach religious beliefs but also nurture a spiritual outlook. When it's functioning the way it should, the church is one such environment.

NURTURING THROUGH THE CHURCH

The church as a center of family life is a strong theme in the conversation of the adult children I interviewed. Apparently, in strong Christian families, church is not only a priority but also a nonnegotiable part of life. Donald Cole's recollections are typical: "Our family was a church-going family," he says. "The organizing principle in the family was, you go to church all the time. At one point in my life I went to church Sunday, Tuesday, and Thursday. Even when I was in high school, I always went to prayer meeting. To me, it seemed the most natural thing in the world. I couldn't imagine not doing it. Going to church was like getting up in the morning and brushing your teeth and going to work. Very early in life we developed a love for it. It wasn't something we sat down and discussed and said, 'Now, let's decide, should we or should we not be a church-going family?' We read the Bible, we prayed, we went to church. Some things were not negotiable."

The impact of Christian community can be so strong that sending kids to church can plant the seeds of genuine spiritual life, even when parents themselves don't go to church. Mary Kay Ash's parents couldn't go to church—her mother had to work on Sundays and her father was ill—but they insisted on sending their daughter to the Tabernacle Baptist Church two blocks from their house. It was there, says Ash, that she got the religious values that have stayed with her throughout her life. "My mother insisted that I take part in all the church's activities for children," she says. "Every Sunday morning I was in Sunday school and church, and every Wednesday afternoon we had Sunbeams, where we learned the Bible and memorized Scripture. I grew up in that atmosphere, and it stuck with me."

Louis McBurney's parents didn't go to church either. His father wasn't interested, and his mother, although a sincere Christian, felt she should stay home with her husband. She did, however, encourage her children to go, and she lived out her faith in a way that made much more of an impression than church attendance alone could have.

"Even though she wasn't actively involved in church, my mother definitely gave us the message of the gospel and the importance of having God in our lives," says McBurney. "Her faith was very important in the development of my faith. I can remember seeing her read the Bible. She talked about her childhood experiences and how important God was in her family and her parents. I knew it was important for her and for me to establish my life around the Scriptures and what God wanted in my life."

MODELING AUTHENTIC FAITH

Important as it is to take children to church, Louis McBurney's mother's example of authentic faith is much more important. David Handley, for example, grew up in a home where going to church, reading the Bible, and praying were a regular part of life. Undoubtedly those disciplines contributed to his spiritual development and his ultimate decision to enter the ministry. But what made the greatest impression on him was the way his parents lived out their Christianity in front of him. Like the way his mother handled her conflict with an old woman in their church.

"Flossie Cottingham and my mother had some real friction because Flossie was apparently holding on to her power in the Sunday school," explains Handley. One Sunday in the middle of winter, when I was about eight years old, I could tell that Mom was really frustrated and ticked off. But after we went home and had lunch, she all of a sudden said, 'Come on, we're going to go over and shovel Flossie's sidewalk. She's too old to do it herself.' I thought it was ridiculous, so I stormed out to the car. When we got to Flossie's, I refused to get out of the car because I thought the whole thing was stupid. But my mom got out of the car and shoveled Flossie's walk. I didn't appreciate it then, but in retrospect one of the greatest gifts my mother gave me was a servant's spirit. My mom was a real servant, a very Christian woman."

Like David Handley, many other adult children say they learned as much, or more, from their parents' spiritual example, than from formal church or family teaching. While overt spiritual instruction is important, a little goes a long way. A positive example is much more effective in the long run. Joan Beck, for example, says she emulated her parents' spiritual values in part because, although they were both very staunch church members, they were never "preachy."

Passing the Hypocrisy Test

Good parents know that when they do give their children moral and spiritual instruction, they should live it out themselves. Children, especially teenagers, have built-in hypocrisy detectors. Nothing turns them off faster than seeing someone, especially a parent, saying one thing and doing another. On the other hand, nothing impresses them more than observing that their parents' actions match their words.

Steve Roskam says that's what impressed him most about his parents. "My parents sent us to Christians camps and took us to church a fair amount, but more than anything, they lived a Christian life," he says. "They were good examples. I would hear stuff in church like, 'You should give part of your money to the Lord,' and we would see them do that. 'You should give part of your time to the Lord,' and we would see them do that. 'You need to love your neighbor,' and we would see them take people in. 'You need to pray,' and we'd see them pray. 'You need to read the Bible,' and they would read the Bible. They weren't hypocritical, living a different life than they said their children should."

Judy Anderson has similar memories of her missionary parents. "My parents transmitted spiritual values through the way they lived their lives," she reflects. "It was obvious they were doing what they were saying. I don't remember my parents talking ill of people. I remember them welcoming a wide range of people with whom they didn't always agree. I remember them being peacemakers. I remember them having devotions every morning. My parents are servants," she continues. "They've been willing to serve and not climb the corporate ladder of success. To me, they epitomize what Christian service is about. They haven't gotten awards, but they've been surrogate parents to hundreds of strangers and people in foreign lands. They pointed the way to the Lord. I never questioned whom they served. They modeled a faith that wasn't something they said, but something they were. And they've always had joy. So I had that model, and I decided very early I wanted to serve the Lord. It was a process, like osmosis."

Modeling Faith Even When It's Hard

Parents' spiritual example is especially powerful when it is lived out in difficult circumstances. O'Ann Steere says she'll never forget a church fight involving, among others, her father's best friend, who was so upset he had decided to take the matter to court. Steere recalls, "My dad went to him and said, 'This is not scriptural. You can't go to court. Would you be willing to submit this to a group at church?' The guy was furious. He said, 'I thought you were my best friend. Don't you understand I'm being ripped off?' I saw my dad willing to sacrifice his friendship with his best friend for what he saw was right, what God expected."

Modeling Faith at Different Levels

Good parents aren't perfect parents. They vary in how far they've progressed in their own spiritual journeys. And with any given couple, one spouse may be farther along than the other. Jay Kesler observes that the example his mother set as a Christian was even more powerful than it might have been otherwise because his father was not a believer until later in life.

"I think my mother modeled Christianity by her kindness and truthfulness," Kesler says. "We understood that Mother was a Christian, and we wished that Dad was, but she never made him an object of our prayers. I think she determined to be the best possible woman she could be. She went along with whatever she could, but when she couldn't, she didn't. We kids were not oblivious to the fact that my dad's friends—

her friends—were out of tune with her Christianity. And we watched how she handled that. Generally speaking, Christians we knew didn't play cards. But my mother would play euchre with dad's friends from work. Though they all smoked, she didn't smoke. Most of them drank beer while playing cards, but she didn't. If someone told an off-color joke, she never laughed. She might not have said anything, but if anyone ever said, 'Ellie, you didn't laugh,' she'd say, 'You know why I didn't laugh.'

"People respected her," he continues. "People came to her for counsel when the chips were really down because they knew she was a Christian. If someone wanted to talk about Christian things, she was available. Her witness was very strong but not harping. I don't think Dad could ever accuse her of being a nag. Her Christianity was strictly positive."

CONVEYING AUTHENTICITY

Good parents manage to convey a spiritual authenticity to their children. David Heim saw that authenticity in his dad's attitude toward his work as a pastor. "As a pastor's kid, you hear your dad give this speech every week about what he believes in, and then you watch and see if it matches the way he lives," Heim explains. "I saw that what my dad preached about on Sundays, about visiting the sick and the widows, he did and did uncomplainingly. He did it feeling it was a privilege. I grew up seeing that as a life worth living, a life of integrity. My dad had a wonderful saying, 'People in the congregation watch me six days a week to find out what I meant on the seventh.' That was very much his piety."

Emphasizing the Essentials
Some parents convey spiritual authenticity by thinking through and communicating to their kids the difference

between Christian essentials and nonessentials. O'Ann Steere's parents did that effectively. "Probably the biggest thing my parents had going for them was the fact that their Christianity was real enough to them that they didn't feel nervous about defending it. They felt God could hang out for himself. They raised three children from scratch, and one they added in from a nightmare background—a foster child who had been raised by a drunken, crazy parent. Even she turned out real stable, so they must have been good parents. But they had a very clear distinction in their minds between what was essential Christianity and what was their preference—and they felt they had a right to demand both. They would say, 'No, God doesn't care what you wear to church, but I do.' So we didn't confuse God's rules with their rules."

Sincerity Goes a Long Way

Harold Best, dean of Wheaton College's Conservatory of Music, grew up in a very strict pastor's family. Although he describes his mother and father as essentially good parents, he says they *didn't* always distinguish between their rules and God's rules. Their Christianity seemed to be defined by rules and guilt. But somehow, the authenticity of his parents' faith came through nonetheless. "I got sick of hearing Dad preach all those years, Sunday after Sunday, and I got sick and tired of living like a preacher's kid when I wanted to go out and drink and smoke," Best says. "But here's what my dad ultimately did for me: he implicitly trusted the Lord. At times when there was no food in the house, he and Mom prayed for food. He trusted the Lord, and the food came. He really, literally believed the promises of Scripture. He deeply believed the Lord and took some very 'bad' churches because he wasn't political about the ministry. He wasn't manipulative or entrepreneurial. He was deeply committed to the Lord Jesus, which is sorely lacking in a good deal of today's public ministries. He never wasted a 'hallelujah' or an 'amen.' They were always meant. He did not vainly repeat the truth. My dad had genuine faith. He was pure. His purity came through. His integrity came through.

"My parents both showed me there was something substantive about the faith, that as strict as the rules were and as much as they imposed them, there was something besides the bath water. There was the baby, which I did not throw out when I threw out the bath water. Somehow they made it clear that God was God, and he's in charge. They made it clear that we are all accountable to him. So the thing they transmitted to me is that whatever the rules are, whatever the rules are worth, God is eminently beyond them."

MODELING SPIRITUAL GROWTH

One of the most powerful ways parents can influence their children's spiritual lives is to model spiritual growth. Children whose parents visibly live out their spiritual journey, acknowledge their own brokenness, claim forgiveness, and open themselves to real change are dramatically affected by the experience.

Fred Barnes recalls that his childhood spiritual training in the mainline Protestant church his parents attended was "breathtakingly superficial." Not surprisingly, Fred dropped out of church entirely in young adulthood. But after his parents retired, moved to Florida, and began attending a church that was undergoing an enthusiastic spiritual awakening, they opened themselves up to a new and more personal kind of Christian experience. Fred and his sister were amazed at the transformation they saw in their parents. "The change permeated my parents," Barnes remembers. "They told us all about what had happened to them, and it was very visible to us. My dad's personality changed, and we became closer. It had a dramatic effect on my life and my sister's. She became a born-again Christian and then helped evangelize me and my wife."

Ron Hutchcraft's parents met God very early in his life, and their spiritual journey set the agenda for his own. When Ron was four years old, his baby brother suddenly died from a kidney illness. Ron's father was devastated, and although he was not a religious man, he decided to start sending Ron to church.

"No one in the family was a Christian at the time," explains Hutchcraft, now a well-known radio and conference speaker. "But my father apparently decided he wanted to do things right with the boy he had left. And his instinct was to take me to church." So every Sunday, Ron's dad would drop him off at the local Baptist congregation, where the little boy attended Sunday school and junior church and soon gave his life to the Lord Jesus Christ. The elder Hutchcraft would sit out in front of the church in their old Nash, smoking a cigarette and reading the paper. One day, the man who taught the men's Sunday school class came out and invited him to join the class. Ron's dad accepted the invitation, began attending regularly, and made a commitment to Christ the following Christmas. Ron's mother made her own commitment not long after. Subsequently, Ron says, his parents grew tremendously in spiritual stature and leadership.

"Because they were first-generation Christians," he says, "my parents appreciated their salvation very deeply. I saw in them a very deep emotional appreciation for what the grace of God had done. They had very soft hearts for the things of God. It wasn't uncommon for me to see my dad shed tears over his salvation. He was easily touched by spiritual things. He loved God's Word, and he had a very marked-up Bible. During every sermon he was underlining and taking notes and trying to understand the Bible. And he was readily convicted of his sin."

By the time he was about ten, Ron's parents were in the

leadership group at church. His father became a trustee, then a deacon, and then chairman of the board of deacons. His mother became president of the women's missionary society. But despite their rapid acquisition of leadership roles, his parents remained very humble. "My father especially modeled humility for me," says Hutchcraft. "He always seemed amazed that he was a deacon or trustee or anything like that. He just felt unworthy of God's grace.

"I think my parents' lives taught me that the achievements that mattered were in a spiritual universe," he continues. "You have to pick what world you're going to achieve in, and I think I got from them the idea that, for me, it would be to serve Jesus Christ."

ACTIVE TEACHING

Parents who model faith earn the right to teach their children the tenets of faith. Good parents do this in a variety of ways. Luis Palau, for example, recalls that his parents surrounded him and his siblings with Christian teaching in both visual and verbal form.

"Even though my dad was a very successful businessman and we lived right on the premises of his business, business wasn't the main topic of conversation in our family," he recalls. "Instead, the conversation revolved around the gospel, evangelism, the Lord's Supper, the church, street meetings, and things of the Lord.

"Our home had Bible passages instead of photographs," he continues. "We had big Bible passages on the walls of the house. When people walked in the door, the first thing they saw was a Bible verse. I also remember we had that famous quotation, 'Christ is the head of this house, a silent listener of every conversation, an invisible guest at every meal.' That was always very touching to me. As I quote it, I get tears in my eyes.

"My parents taught us to memorize Scripture verses. Memorizing a verse every Sunday was as much a part of life as breakfast, lunch, and dinner. They encouraged a healthy competitiveness to see who could memorize Scripture most accurately. I still have a few old Bibles that were prizes for Bible memorization."

The Bible as the Basis of Teaching

Many children of good parents cite their parents' biblical teaching as a strength of their spiritual training—and upbringing. Retired attorney Gerhardt Jersild, for example, recalls that biblical instruction was a high priority for his Danish immigrant parents. "My father made certain that we got a Christian education," he recalls. "We had not only confirmation instruction in the church but also Bible reading when we were all at the table at home. I remember he brought me to his study one night and said I should read the Bible from the very start to the finish. Since our Bible was in Danish, that was not very easy. My mother had the greatest part in our spiritual training, though, because my father, as a minister in charge of four congregations, was gone a lot. She was the one who had us read the Bible most of the time. I have a dear recollection of one evening, when my father was away for an evening service, and she had us memorize Danish verses from the Bible. One of them I could recite in Danish [he reads from his Danish Bible and then translates]: 'Be a rock of safety where I always can come for help.'"

Drawing on Daily Life for Object Lessons

Good parents use the events of daily living as practical examples of spiritual truth, as Grace Ketterman's father did. Every spring, he would take his young daughter to see all the newborn animals—baby pigs, calves, colts, and chickens. One time, while watching a chick pecking its way through its shell, young Ketterman wanted to help it out. But her father gently pulled back her hand, explaining, "No, God made that little chick so it has to peck its own way out or it will be too weak to live."

"My dad used so many everyday episodes in a casual, natural fashion to teach us about the power of God," reflects Ketterman. "He used to say he could read a sermon by walking through a wheat field, and he did. He knew that he and God were partners, that without God's help and his own work, that field of wheat wouldn't be there. He so vividly portrayed that incredible partnership that I couldn't doubt it. It was marvelous spiritual training."

The Power of Stories

Good parents know the power of stories in conveying spiritual values. They tell their children stories of faith—from their own lives and the lives of spiritual heroes and heroines. They read their children Bible stories and spiritually oriented books. They let their children overhear stories of spiritual adventure.

Janet Getz's spiritual life began as a small child, when, as she puts it, she was "captured by the stories." "I had a children's Bible," she says, "and I remember sitting in my bedroom at night and looking at the pictures and reading the wonderful stories. When I was very little, my parents used to sit and read the stories to me."

Gregg Roeber's father used to tell a remarkable story that made an enormous impression on him as a child growing up on a Colorado ranch. "My father came from a household in which his parents constantly fought with each other. As a junior-high student, my dad would pray that his mother and father wouldn't break up—and that his beloved dog, who was getting older, would not die until he was out of high school and old enough to be on his own. As it turned out, the dog died the day after he graduated from high school. My dad said that, while it might seem like a trivial kind of thing to be praying about, for him it was a heartfelt prayer. It was obviously very important to him. And it was a stunning story to me."

Nancy Swider-Peltz' mother used to read to her and her brothers every day, usually Bible stories or Christian books. "The one I remember most was a big fat children's Bible story book," she says. "And we had these Bible stories in comic form. We just loved those. We'd go through them hundreds of times."

Luis Palau's parents made a point of exposing their children to stories of great Christians, often the biographies of missionaries who gave their lives for their faith. "Our parents made missionaries heroes in our eyes," says Palau. "Martyrs were our heroes. In my heart, I still feel missionaries are the greatest heroes, especially the missionaries who gave their lives for the cause of Christ. Even though I was born in Argentina, a country considered a mission field, my parents gave me a burden for missions. As children, we got a burden for China, Africa, and all the countries of the world. That came from my parents; there's no question about it."

NURTURE, DON'T FORCE, SPIRITUAL VALUES

It's a classic pattern. Children who grow up in religious families often rebel against their parent's faith—and then return to the church after a period of sowing their wild oats. Even many Christian leaders fit this pattern. But in an era of drug abuse and AIDS, sowing one's wild oats can be lethal. And many of the adult children I talked to said it doesn't have to happen that way. The secret, they say, is for parents to nurture spiritual values without the heavyhandedness that almost necessitates rebellion. They say that, while their parents were unabashed about exposing them to religious and moral teaching—through the church and in the home—they didn't force it.

Take going to church, for example. While most of the interviewees say going to church wasn't a topic of negotiation in their families, neither was it an opportunity for spiritual bludgeoning. "Church was never crammed down our throats," explains Jon Ebersole. "It was just part of life. We went to church every Sunday, but my parents didn't get hyper about it. They just did it and took us along."

Wise parents take a similar approach to family devotions or other forms of spiritual instruction. They incorporate them as a routine part of family life without making an issue of it. That's what Keri Menconi's parents did. "We read Bible stories at night, and my parents would talk with us about Christian things," says Menconi. "But my dad has made it a point not to push anything on us. We were a Christian family, and we just came to believe in Christianity. There was no reason to rebel against it."

Resist the Temptation to Coerce

Good parents teach their children moral and spiritual values lovingly, not threateningly. They offer their kids rational explanations for family rules based on those values. While they carefully explain the consequences of breaking the rules, they don't invoke God as the Big Enforcer in the Sky. They resist the temptation to coerce their children into faith, or civilized behavior, by portraying God as Big Daddy with the Spiritual Paddle. "In my family," says Julie Ravencroft, "religion wasn't forced or used as a weapon or disciplinary action or mirror to show how we didn't measure up. We grew up knowing that God loved us, that Jesus loved us, that angels watched over us. Spiritual values were just all around my life. We had prayers before dinner, thanking God for the food.

Prayers before bedtime. The routine was, we'd get tucked in, and Mom and Dad would pray with us. If we were scared or upset, if we couldn't sleep because something scary was under the bed, they'd remind us that Jesus was watching over us, that his angels were with us, and that we were okay. So the way they introduced God into our lives was through loving and caring."

Gretchen Ziegenhals says her parents' rational, practical approach to teaching moral and spiritual values was a major factor in her decision to incorporate those values in her own life. "Some of my friends' parents taught a sense of morality through threats. They would say to their kids, 'If I ever catch you drinking beer, I'll . . .' My parents weren't like that. They certainly provided a strong structure of beliefs and right and wrong, but they never rammed it down our throats. It was always explained in a rational manner. I remember hearing them talk about their views on premarital sex, for example. It wasn't like, 'You'll die and rot in hell if you do this,' but, 'Here are four or five reasons why we don't think it's a good idea.' They gave very practical reasons as well as moral reasons, and they gave the reasons in a useful, open manner. And the reasons made sense. I appreciated that."

Accentuate the Positive

Good parents seem to understand that, while God asks us to count the cost of our beliefs, children need positive experiences to bind them to the church and to the life of faith. Wise parents immerse their children in a warm, sensory-rich church life, for example. They make the church a center of their social life. They take their children to churches that offer them an opportunity to make friends—with other children, other godly adults, and with God himself. They portray God in his full personality, not just a God of justice, but a God who loves and cares for his children. And they exude a sense of joy in their own faith. Perhaps that's why so many children of good parents have such warm memories of church and of the God of their childhoods.

For Donald Cole, the experience of worship will always be linked in his mind and heart with the sights and sounds and smells of his childhood church. "My earliest memories are saturated with recollections of times in church," he says. "I remember the building. I loved the building, even as a kid. And the goblets for communion; I can still remember them. They were enormous things with wooden lids on them. We'd pass the wine around and lift the wooden lid on the goblet and the place would be filled with the aroma of wine—real wine, not grape juice. We had the real stuff, great-smelling stuff. I can recall we'd always look for an excuse to sit next to my aunt. She had one of those furs with the fox heads on them, and we'd snap the jaws on that all during church. And, of course, we'd get to put the dollar bill in the big velvet bags." Like Donald Cole's mother and father, good parents know, perhaps unconsciously, the power of the senses in binding children to the church community.

Church as Social Center

Good parents also know the importance of making church a social center of their lives. Dick Chase, for example, says that he has never had anything but pleasant associations with church, mainly because church was the center of his family's social life. "I had friends at church from the age of five or six," he recalls. Jody Hedberg says that, as a teenager in a small Indiana town, continuing in a life of faith was made a lot easier by the fact that her high-school Sunday school class was the "in" place to be. "It was a social center," she says, "and we had a great teacher who let us talk about dating and encouraged us to work out our Christianity in our day-to-day living."

Giving the Whole Picture

Whether they develop their view of God from church or from their parents or from both, the God that children meet early in life is often the God they will live with, or run away from, when they grow older. That's why it's so important to portray God in his full personality. God is a God of justice, yes, but he is also a God of love and grace and mercy. Madeleine L'Engle says that, thanks to her parents, she has never had to struggle with her image of God. "I think the best thing my parents did was give me a God of love," she explains. "I knew I didn't have to win points to gain God's love. I had it. So many people grow up with a punitive God, an angry God. I never had that angry God. I always had a God of love. And that was wonderful. For that alone, I'll be grateful to them forever."

While it's good to give children a positive view of God and the church, we need to remember that the Christian life isn't always pleasant. We are aliens in this world. Kids need to learn that.

Kids do need to learn that being a Christian means being part of a minority, sometimes a ridiculed, even persecuted, minority. But that doesn't mean Christian parents can't make the life of faith attractive, that they can't portray it as an exciting adventure.

The Adventure of Faith

Luis Palau's family was part of what was, at the time, a tiny and much-maligned Protestant minority in Argentina. It would have been understandable if he had been tempted to reject the faith that made the neighbors gather in front of the Palau house to "exorcise" it from demons. But because his parents exhibited such joy and took such pleasure in their faith, their children did too. "My parents made us feel very comfortable and proud to be evangelical Christians," Palau says. "We were persecuted, and yet we were unashamed to be persecuted for the cause of Jesus Christ. We were a despised minority, but we never felt inferior because of it. In fact, we felt a surge of adrenaline because we were a tiny minority in our community. My parents taught us that the gospel was a blessing to people. So even though we were a total minority, we had a sense of victory."

BE OPEN TO DISCUSSION

Parents who manage to inculcate spiritual values that stick tend to be parents who are open to discussion, who can listen to their kids' questions without feeling threatened. Like O'Ann Steere's parents. "They were pretty unshockable," she observes. "We could tell them anything. I remember having a discussion with my father, for example, about whether God created sex for recreation or procreation. Most of my friends couldn't have discussions like that with their parents. I said, 'I think God made sex to be fun.' And my dad said, 'No, he made it for procreation and made it fun so we'd do it.' The answer wasn't important, but the discussion was incredible."

Gretchen Ziegenhals's parents, instead of panicking when she came home from high school and declared, "My friend Bill says there's no God," began what turned out to be a long series of theological discussions. Those discussions stood her in good stead when Ziegenhals went off to college, majored in religion, and found that most of her professors didn't believe in God. "They were just interested in studying Freud, Nietzsche, and existential philosophers and calling it religion. I was so confused and frustrated! I ended up calling my parents a lot." Ziegenhals eventually reaffirmed her faith and even ended up going to seminary. It's unlikely she would have done either, she says, if her parents hadn't continued talking and listening.

Mary O'Connor recalls that adolescence, a period when many kids reject their parents' beliefs, was the time when she and her mother had some of their best conversations about spiritual things. "I was at an age where I was starting to question a lot of things, and she was always available to talk about it," says O'Connor. "I was questioning the very existence of God, and we talked about morality. I remember thinking sometimes that I knew more than she did, but that didn't bother her in the least. She respected me enough that she felt I would be able to work it through. She never got hysterical about it, which I really admired in her. I think about it even now when I'm responding to my kids. I try not to fly off the handle at things that might shock me or make me feel afraid."

Like Mary O'Connor's mother, good parents avoid giving their children the impression that it's somehow dangerous to ask questions. Janet Getz is a person of strong faith, but she says her spiritual journey might have taken a very different turn if her parents had panicked as soon as she began questioning the claims of Christianity: "We were living in Egypt when I was in high school, and perhaps because I was living in a Muslim community and going to school with fifty-four different nationalities, I began to question what's true. It seems that in some families the parents say, 'The Bible says this and that's it. Don't even think about it.' But in our family, it wasn't dangerous to think. Honestly seeking and wanting to know and understand was allowed."

Good parents nurture spiritual values in their children's lives. Although their children are ultimately responsible for accepting the truth of those values, wise parents know some of the secrets of passing on their faith in a way that will stick. They expose their children to a community of faith, usually the local church. They live as examples of authentic faith. They open themselves to spiritual growth and allow their children to observe that process, even if it means exposing their own imperfection and brokenness. They teach their children the tenets of faith—verbally, visually, and metaphorically. They know and use the power of stories in making faith come alive. They gently guide their children into understanding spiritual truth instead of forcing them into rebellion. They do what they can to give their children positive experiences with the church, to portray God's love as well as his wrath, and to show the Christian life as the adventure it can be.

It's possible to raise good children without consciously and consistently exposing them to spiritual values. It's even possible to raise children who eventually embrace the life of faith without making a special effort to teach them Christian precepts. Many productive, well-rounded Christians came to faith in adulthood. But children who grow up living and observing a life of faith have an advantage. Just ask Gretchen Ziegenhals. "When I was in high school," she says, "I had a lot of friends who told me, 'Oh, it's easy for you to believe in God because you grew up believing in God.' It's true. I grew up living and breathing faith. Of course I went through times of doubt and moments of asking, 'Is there really someone up there?' But I'm so grateful for the start my parents gave me. The fact that faith was in my blood makes faith so much easier now. Not necessarily qualitatively better, but so much easier."

Give your children a spiritual advantage. Make it easy for them not only to believe in God but also to want to serve him. It's one of the secrets of good parenting.

• FIVE •

Understand the Secrets of Balanced Discipline

I'm not sure whether my parents were strict or not strict. I was spanked with my mother's silver hairbrush. Of course, today, that would be considered child abuse, I suppose, which I think is silly.

Madeleine L'Engle

My parents set standards, but I never had a sense they were enforced arbitrarily or meanly. They gave a reasonable explanation for the discipline. I never had a sense it was irrational or violent or out of control or without reasons.

Timothy Johnson

I have a choleric temperament, and it showed. So my parents let me cool off by locking me in the bathroom. That wasn't the smartest move because I let the water run. The most effective thing was to stand me in a corner. If I fussed, I stayed another fifteen minutes. It did me good. I cooled off from all the anger and explosiveness. I thought ugly and bitter thoughts, and then my mind would sort out. Today I have nothing but great love, respect, honor, and thankfulness for my parents.

Luis Palau

PUT YOURSELF IN my shoes: you're interviewing people for a book about parenting, looking for common threads in the ways good parents raise their children. You find lots of them. You start feeling pretty confident. You begin to believe there really are some clear trends, some right answers. But when you start asking grown children of good parents to describe their parents' disciplinary style, the responses are all over the map. Consider these reflections from Donald Cole, radio pastor for Moody Radio Network, for example: "Mother never controlled her boys. She was always amused by us. She loved little boys, and no matter how awful we may have been, Mother thought it was funny. She really did. I do not recall having been spanked three times in my life. I can remember, when I was about twelve years old, Mother thought I had become really quite outrageous, and she was trying to spank me with a pancake turner. We both ended up laughing. That was the way it always was.

"I don't recall discipline. I don't recall my parents observing all kinds of rules and regulations, even though my father was, in many ways, a very tough customer. He'd been a Marine Corps drill sergeant on Paris Island. He'd been a sheriff in Jackson County, Missouri. He was part-owner of a bank, and when the bank was invaded by bank robbers, one of them fired a gun at my dad. Dad shot and killed the robber immediately. Shot the throat out of the other one. The third one came in and threw up his hands. But Dad did not spank us. He never yelled at us. But when Dad said jump, we jumped. When he said do this, we did that. We did not disobey. And he rarely gave us any orders. He didn't pick on us. He didn't nag us. And neither did my mother. This doesn't mean they would have tolerated rotten behavior. They wouldn't.

"We never rebelled," Cole continues. "It never occurred to us to rebel. Rebel against what? I suppose my parents' ideas would have been called liberal by some people. I heard a preacher on the radio today encouraging people to spank their kids. He quoted the proverb, 'He who spares the rod hates his child,' calling for corporal punishment on the basis of a few texts in Proverbs. My parents would have sneered at that. They didn't think you had to beat on kids to make them behave."

Other adult children of good parents had other memories. Steve Roskam recalls, "My parents were definitely toward the strict side. We were spanked. We had a curfew. We got the belt if we were bad. What evangelical Christianity said was right and wrong at the time dictated how we were raised."

Keri Menconi's experience was very different from Steve's. "My parents weren't disciplinarians at all. Discipline wasn't a big thing. I never had a set curfew. They pretty much let us do our own thing. I got spanked maybe six times in the whole time I was growing up."

Fred Barnes remembers, "My parents had requirements. They were not laissez-faire, progressive, or modern parents in any way whatsoever. They would never allow my sister and me out roaming. It was a fairly strict upbringing."

Louis McBurney's parents were more like Menconi's. "My parents were lenient," he says. "I don't remember many rules or regulations. I'm not sure I can remember a time when they didn't allow me to do something I asked permission to do."

All these comments come from the mouths of responsible adults. They're achievers. They love and respect their parents. But they are the products of vastly different philosophies and styles of discipline.

So what is the *right* philosophy, the right style, of discipline?

The way you answer that question depends on many variables: when and where you were born, how you were raised yourself, what parenting books you read, what child-development experts you believe.

Discipline is the focus of much of the current writing about parenting. It's also the subject of much discussion among parents and adults who work with children. So why haven't we reached more of a consensus on the subject?

I don't know the answer to that question. But I have come to this conclusion: the disciplinary styles of good parents have some important common factors. But those common principles, summarized in the following pages, have very little to do with strictness versus leniency.

TREAT YOUR CHILDREN
WITH RESPECT AND LOVE

Ron Hutchcraft is a conservative guy—a real straight arrow. A graduate of Moody Bible Institute, Hutchcraft has spent most of his adult life in some form of ministry. He's also an achiever: valedictorian of his class, former regional director of a large youth-outreach organization, radio and conference speaker, head of his own national ministry. He's not the sort of guy you picture when you think of the likely product of a permissive home. But Hutchcraft describes his parents, and his dad in particular, as quite lenient.

"My dad was a pretty soft-hearted man," Hutchcraft explains. "I think the death of my brother really made it tough for him to spank or punish me. I don't know that I invited their discipline. I was a pretty good kid. I got some spankings, but not a lot. I think their disappointment was discipline enough for me most of the time. Actually, it was more of a preventive factor, a deterrent. I felt, 'Don't disappoint these people.'"

Don't disappoint these people. Repeatedly, grown children of good parents told me that what kept them in line was not the threat of a spanking or grounding or loss of some privilege, but a reluctance to disappoint their parents. As Hutchcraft says, "One of the greatest things parents have going for them is to love a kid in such a way that the kid doesn't want to disappoint them. 'You believe in me, trust me, love me, generously meet my needs. How can I stab you in the back? I don't want to hurt somebody like that.'"

Good parents, it seems, have earned a degree of love and respect that makes it difficult for their children to hurt them. Consider Mary O'Connor's father, for example. "If he erred," O'Connor says, "it was in being too gentle. Still, we wouldn't think of crossing him because we just never wanted to disappoint him. He expected us to be good, and that was the way it was. I compare that to other parents who would be very strict and a little harsh, and I think they got worse results."

The strong desire children of good parents have to avoid disappointing their parents almost eliminates the question of whether or not to spank. Gregg Roeber reflects, "I was never beaten. I can't remember more than two or three times in my entire childhood that my father gave me even a swat. And that was for explicit disobedience, something I had been told was dangerous and did anyway. But that was nothing. It was the disapproval that was most crushing."

Elaine Kirk echoes Roeber's experience. "I don't recall ever being spanked. And if my parents would ever scold me, the scolding wouldn't hurt as much as the fact I had done something to prompt it."

Good parents know that if they've earned the love and respect of their children, even the most gentle of reproofs is a more than adequate deterrent to further misbehavior. In fact, a gentle reproof is more effective than a harsh one, as David Heim's father knew. "My dad could register disappointment with you in such a heartfelt way," says Heim, "that even though what he said was very mild, you felt terrible."

ASSURE YOUR KIDS OF YOUR UNCONDITIONAL LOVE

As much as Ron Hutchcraft wanted to please his parents, he says he never felt theirs was a "performance love," that they'd love him more if he obeyed and achieved. As much as Brenda Weaver wanted to avoid disappointing her parents, she says she has never felt a need to prove anything to them. "Disappointing my parents is very painful to me," she admits. "But if I mess up, I don't feel scared. I know they have a lot of trust in me. I don't feel this urge that I have to be successful."

Instead of forcibly bending their children to their will—which may have the unintended result of breaking their spirits or forcing them into rebellion—good parents live their lives in ways that help their kids admire them, love them, and want to please them. But good parents also make sure their children know that their love is unconditional.

"I don't think my parents ever withheld any form of love," says Lowell Olberg about his Norwegian immigrant parents. "None of us were exactly goody-goodies. We'd go out and do a little mischief. But it wasn't like, 'Hey, you disappointed me and therefore I'm going to lord it over you or use psychological warfare, you bad boy.' It wasn't like that at all. It was just that you knew that if you didn't do what was right, you would disappoint them, and you just didn't want to disappoint them."

GIVE YOUR KIDS FREEDOM WITHIN LIMITS

It was a funny thing. When I asked Jon Ebersole about his parents' strengths, one of the first things he mentioned was the degree of freedom they gave him. "My parents provided a lot of leniency in our family," he said. "For the most part, I was allowed to do what I wanted. We didn't hear a lot of, 'Do this, don't do that.' There weren't many rules." But later in our conversation, Ebersole mentioned that his family was Mennonite: "Because we were Christian and Mennonite, we just didn't do certain things. We stayed home at night. We didn't drink. We didn't dance." When I pointed out to him that a lot of people would view his Mennonite upbringing as rather strict, the opposite of lenient in fact, he acknowledged the point but insisted that his parents managed to instill a sense of freedom. Somehow, for reasons he couldn't quite explain, he never felt he was under their thumb. Others cited a similar sense of freedom.

Take Keri Menconi, for example. "My parents somehow gave us a sense of freedom, even though they were fairly overprotective of us in some ways," she recalls. "They didn't want us seeing sleazy movies that my friends were able to see, and they wanted to keep tabs on where I was going and what I was doing. It sounds paradoxical, but they gave me overprotection yet freedom. I never had a set curfew. We would just discuss where I was going and what I was doing. If I was late, they weren't waiting at the door to punish me. They were reasonable. We children did have to go to church on Sunday mornings, for example, but we didn't have to go to Sunday school. It really helped that they weren't making it mandatory. We ended up getting involved, and it turned out to be something fun we wanted to do. I think their disciplinary style made us self-motivated."

Then there's Andy Tiebert. Now a fundraiser for a large social service agency, he grew up in the seventies, when many of his peers were doing drugs and generally rebelling against the constraints of the previous generation. But Andy never felt particularly vulnerable to peer pressure. "I never felt I had to push the edges because I always felt I had plenty of latitude," he says. "It wasn't that I was suppressing something. I just didn't feel the need to go out and do wild and crazy things because I always felt my parents treated me with respect."

Freedom to Make Choices

What's curious about the freedom these children of good parents describe is that they often don't know how their parents communicated that sense of freedom—and often, it was freedom within very set limits. But it's clear that good parents give their children choices whenever they can. That's what Louis McBurney's parents did. McBurney says one of the hallmarks of the way his parents raised him was their confidence in him and the freedom they gave him to explore. He points to the way his father handled his decision-making process about a career as an example. The elder McBurney made no secret of the fact that he had wanted his son to attend the naval academy. He worked through their congressman to get young Louis an appointment, but when Louis was disqualified because he wore glasses, his father accepted the situation with grace. "He gave me the freedom to choose and do anything I wanted," notes McBurney, "and what I wanted was to go into drama. I'm pretty sure Dad wasn't real excited about that, but he never refused permission or told me he thought I ought to do something different. He was accepting and supportive. I think he was relieved when I changed my mind, but because both my parents saw me as gifted and capable of making good decisions and choices, they trusted my judgment about things and encouraged me to do whatever I wanted to do."

Freedom to Talk

Keri Menconi was thinking hard about her parents' disciplinary style and why their leniency was so effective with her, while the well-meaning strictness of some of her friends' parents seemed to have backfired. She wasn't sure, she said, but she thought it had something to do with the fact that her parents were always willing to talk—and to listen.

"I have a friend whose father is a pastor and a real

disciplinarian," she said. "He's so strict that my friend has a hard time approaching him. He won't hear her out at all. He doesn't let his kids talk to him. His word is final, and his kids can't speak to him after he gives it. He doesn't respect them as people. My parents were permissive, but we could always tell them how we felt."

Janet Getz's parents were less permissive than Menconi's, but she remembers and appreciates that talking was okay in her family too. "If something happened," she says, "we would talk about what happened and why. We talked about what to do next, what choices to make. And my parents would see that we followed through. They were very consistent about that. They were probably on the strict side, but not authoritarian in the sense of, 'You did this, now go to your room, close the door, you can't talk about it.' For me, it was a good balance."

GIVE APPROPRIATE CONSEQUENCES

Janet Getz remembers not only her parents' openness to talk about her mistakes and misdeeds but also their quiet way of teaching that wrong actions—even when they've been discussed and forgiven—have consequences. "Sometimes we were spanked," she says, "but usually our wrongdoing would have some natural consequences. When I threw all the silverware on the floor because I was mad, I had to wash it all and set the table."

Other children of good parents say that's the way it was in their families too. Grace Ketterman recalls, "When my father said, 'Do this job,' I knew I had to do it sooner or later or there would be a creative disciplinary action. If I failed to do my job because I preferred to read, all reading material would be lifted for a few days. I remember once I forgot to do my jobs in the evening, and he awakened me late at night, and I had to do a job in the dark when it was late and cold. He didn't berate me or call me names or put me down. It was just, 'This is your job, you failed to do it, and here are the consequences.'"

Terry Tochihara, a telecommunications company executive who grew up in a Japanese-American family in Colorado, recalls that her parents took an especially creative approach to teaching their children about consequences: the kids had to decide their own consequences. "When we did something wrong," Terry says, "it was up to us to determine how to fix it. We had to think it through ourselves. With four children in the family, for example, we were always fighting. But rather than my mom or dad stopping the fight and telling us what to do, we had to negotiate it among ourselves. We knew the fight was wrong, but we also knew we were expected to solve it ourselves. I think that style led to creative thinking."

WHAT GOOD PARENTS, BOTH STRICT AND LENIENT, HAVE IN COMMON

I was intrigued and puzzled. Modern child-development experts talk about giving children boundaries, setting limits, having firm guidelines. But so many of the adult children I was interviewing—children who had grown up to be responsible, well-adjusted adults—were describing their parents as lenient, bordering on permissive. They were talking about childhoods characterized by great freedom and few limits. Others—equally responsible, well-adjusted adults—talked about unusually strict parents. But whether their parents were very strict or very lenient seemed to have little relation to how the adult children evaluated the effectiveness of the parenting they received. Children of lenient parents appreciated their leniency. Children of strict parents, for the most part, appreciated their strictness—at least in retrospect. Confusing. But as I took a closer look at individual stories, I started seeing some common factors where I didn't expect to find them. Both strict and lenient parents seemed to make their disciplinary decisions with some common criteria.

GOOD PARENTS GEAR DISCIPLINE TO THE INDIVIDUAL CHILD

One of the strong themes running through my conversations with grown children who believe they had good parents was the parents' knowledge and acceptance of their kids as individuals—and their ability to adjust their parenting style accordingly. In no area was this more true than in disciplinary style.

David Handley, now pastor of a large Presbyterian church, describes his parents as lenient almost to the point of permissiveness. They gave him much more freedom than he would ever give his kids, he says. But, he adds, his parents' leniency was based in part on their knowledge of him as a person. Some kids might have needed more limits; Dave's parents seemed to understand that he needed, and could handle, a lot of autonomy.

"They seemed to be keyed into the fact that I was a pretty self-directed kid," he muses. "They seemed to know how to give me a long enough leash so I could monitor myself. I think they perceived me as somebody with a very sensitive conscience. I knew what my family's values were, and the pain of conscience was there to be the end of the leash for me."

O'Ann Steere's parents were very intentional about gearing their decisions to their kids' individual needs and personalities, so much so that the children sometimes saw those decisions as unfair. "Their rules were geared to children, not to justice," says Steere. "We got to see movies on an approval basis, for example, and I remember one time my younger sister got approval to go see *West Side Story* and I didn't. I was very frustrated. 'What! I'm the oldest one. What do you mean Marsha can go and I can't?' But they based their decision on who could go and who couldn't on our individual personalities." Needless to say, Steere and her sisters didn't always appreciate their parents' assessments of them as individuals and their resulting decisions. But they do now.

GOOD PARENTS GEAR DISCIPLINE TO THEIR PARTICULAR ENVIRONMENT

Just as good parents don't put any more limits on their children than they individually need, they likewise don't put any more limits on their children than their environment requires. One of the reasons so many of the interviewees grew up with so much freedom, I've decided, is that they were raised in times and places that allowed for much freedom. Several of the grown children I talked with, for example, were raised on farms, which can sometimes offer an environment of relative freedom without the multitude of harmful outside influences often found in more urban settings. As Elaine Kirk observes about her upbringing on a midwestern farm, "We always had plenty of companionship and plenty of work to do. Maybe that kept us out of trouble."

In some cases, the tightknit social fabric of a small town can allow parents to be more lenient than they might be in another setting, because they know their values will be supported. "I had a sense of great freedom growing up," says Jody Hedberg. "But it was a small town. Everyone knew everyone. You couldn't do anything because someone was bound to see it and would tip off your parents."

Some environments, of course, are so dangerous or morally threatening that giving kids too much freedom would be an act of outright neglect. Even the most careful, well-meaning parents living in some urban neighborhoods, for example, have to fight hard to protect their children from the powerful lure of gangs and drugs. But the inner city isn't the only environment that might call for a stricter parenting style.

Gregg Roeber says that the Colorado ranching community he grew up in is evidence of that. "My parents were pretty strict," he says, "certainly in comparison with the way some of my schoolmates were raised. By the time they got into high school, for example, many kids in our rural community were heavily into liquor, the drug of choice in those days. And there were many premarital pregnancies. I think my parents realized this could be a dangerous kind of situation. If we didn't make the right kinds of choices, we could so thoroughly foul up the rest of our lives that there would be no recovery." Since it's impossible to generalize about the dangers or benefits inherent to particular kinds of environments—be they urban, suburban, or rural—good parents carefully assess their own environment and adjust their limits accordingly.

GOOD PARENTS GIVE REASONS FOR THEIR RULES

O'Ann Steere remembers that her parents always had reasons for their rules. "I didn't always agree with the reasons," she says "but they always had them. For example, when we were young, we weren't allowed to go see *Dr. Zhivago*. My parents had gone to see the movie with our pastor and came back and said, 'The trouble with this movie is, you wish for a man to commit adultery.' Our position was, 'We know people commit adultery.' But they said, 'You're too young to go to a movie where they manipulate your emotions to want someone to commit adultery.' That taught us to make choices with some sense behind them. Not that we always thought their theory was right, but at least they always had a theory. They didn't say, 'No, because I said so.' I think that approach is tremendously frustrating to children because it doesn't teach them anything."

Steere's comments reflect the experience of many adult

children. Whether their parents had many rules or only a few, adult children who appreciated their parents say they had logical reasons for the limits they set. Grace Ketterman's observation is typical: "My father was particularly gifted with logic," she recalls. "Whatever he did or wanted us to do, he had a reason for it."

Having logic behind your rules isn't particularly helpful, of course, unless you communicate those reasons to your kids— without lecturing or haranguing. Being open to questions helps a lot. "If I didn't understand a rule," says Madeleine L'Engle, "I asked my parents and was told, reasonably, why they had made it. We can't get away from rules. But sometimes when you're in a very, very rigid atmosphere where the rules don't seem to be for any particular purpose, they're not liberating. They're just rules. They're scary. You're not allowed to ask questions. I was allowed to ask questions."

The most difficult rules for children to accept are those that set them apart from their peers. You may never enjoy the satisfaction of hearing your child, especially a teenager, admit he or she understands or agrees with the rationale behind such a rule, but it's critically important that you have one, one you really believe in yourself. Just ask Nancy Swider-Peltz, who became a four-time Olympic athlete thanks in part to the encouragement and rules of her parents. "My parents were extremely strict compared to other people," she says. "But by my middle teens, I started liking the fact that my parents treated me differently. I started understanding why they did what they did, seeing it would be ultimately for my good. I think I never needed to rebel because they gave us very mature reasons for their rules. They gave us logical answers. When I asked them why I couldn't stay overnight at slumber parties, their reasons were, 'You're in athletics. You're in school. When you stay overnight, you don't get enough sleep. It's not good for you.' I think children need to see why their parents make the decisions they do and understand that there is something different in the way they are being strict and that makes it okay."

GOOD PARENTS ARE GENTLE BUT FIRM

I remember my brother saying once that there are two kinds of households in the world: those where you're not allowed to wear shoes in the house and those where you must wear shoes in the house. In his experience, at least, parents tend to be very firm in their belief in the importance of wearing or not wearing shoes.

Whatever their rules, it seems that good parents are firm about enforcing them. At least that's what grown children of good parents reported. The word "firm" popped up over and over again in my interviews. The things that their parents were firm about varied tremendously. But that didn't seem to matter. And the number of rules also didn't matter. If parents explained the reasons behind the rules—"You shouldn't wear shoes in the house because they might get dirt on the carpet," or conversely, "You must wear shoes in the house to protect your feet"—and they were firmly but not harshly enforced, kids seemed to respect them.

Timothy Johnson observes, "My parents' disciplinary style was gently firm. They established a sense of right and wrong, but they were neither strict nor lenient. I guess maybe the word to describe them is 'concerned.' They were aware of what was going on in our lives, wanted to know what was going on, expressed their opinions a lot, but it never felt overbearing in the sense of being strict. Yet it wasn't lenient in the sense of not caring."

The basis of the gentle firmness exhibited by effective parents seems to be a core confidence in themselves and the relationship they've established with their children. These parents aren't worried about a temporary loss of favor in their children's eyes. "If our parents disciplined us," recalls Jay

Kesler, "they didn't try to win our friendship back as if they were worried about losing it. They expressed none of that weak seeking of approval from children. We cried until we were through crying, until the discipline sunk in. If we went to bed in tears, my dad would come in later and explain why we had been disciplined. We had to acknowledge what happened, and he would stay at it until we understood what had happened."

In talking with children of good parents, I got the impression that in some cases, it didn't really matter all that much what their parents were being firm about; it just seems to be important for kids to bump up against some limits, to learn that sometimes in life they have to conform their behavior to external expectations. But firmness is helpful only when it's applied consistently. Good parents don't enforce the rules one time and ignore them another. "My parents were very consistent in their strictness," reflects Nancy Swider-Peltz. "They didn't say one thing one time and change their mind the next time. We knew what to expect on a day-to-day basis. At times that could be frustrating. We knew certain things we couldn't do because we knew how consistent our parents were."

Sometimes it's better to be consistent than it is to be right. As Doug Anderson observes about his parents, "They may have been wrong sometimes, but at least we knew exactly what they were going to do."

Children derive a tremendous sense of security from their parents' consistency, as Ruth Smith discovered in observing the inconsistency of some of her friends' parents. "I took my parents' complete predictability for granted until I met people who never knew what their parents might do," she says. "They might throw them out of the house or beat them or never speak to them or be really forgiving. They might totally overreact to a small thing, like being a little bit late for a curfew, and then the next time say, 'Oh, it's no big deal.' But my parents were totally consistent."

GOOD PARENTS DISCIPLINE WITH LOVE

"I remember being spanked only once as a child," recalls Gretchen Ziegenhals. "It was a spontaneous whack, not a, 'Sit down, get the belt!' kind of thing that I heard about from my friends. I was talking about this and about how to discipline a child at a family gathering, and my father said something interesting. He said, 'We never really used the word "discipline." We liked the phrase, "loving you into direction." We always felt that if you involved children in purposeful activities, you could channel their energies in a creative direction. It wasn't discipline or teaching you to respect authority, although that came with it.' In retrospect, I appreciated hearing that phrase. I thought, *Oh yes, that's what they did.*"

Nancy Swider-Peltz's parents were very different from Ziegenhals's in many ways. They were much stricter; they had many rules and regulations. But like Ziegenhals's parents' discipline, their discipline was characterized by love. "There was a real strictness to their discipline," says Swider-Peltz, "but it was done with such love. That's probably the catch. Strictness has to be done out of love. We knew our parents wanted the best for us, that they took a very personal interest in our well-being and happiness. They didn't want to do anything purposefully to make us sad. They always reassured us that they cared and loved and respected us."

GOOD PARENTS HAVE POSITIVE EXPECTATIONS

I've often observed that kids tend to behave the way their parents expect them to: when parents communicate a sense of disapproval and distrust, a sense that they believe their kids are likely to misbehave given half a chance, that's precisely what's likely to happen. But when parents communicate approval and trust, when they let it be known that they *expect* their children to do the right thing, they generally do.

Listen to these children of good parents reflect about their parents' expectations. Joan Beck says, "I don't remember anything you would call disciplinary. My parents communicated, 'This is the way we do things.' And we didn't see any need to violate their expectations." Nancy Tecson recalls, "I can't really think of any discipline from my parents except we felt they expected us to do or not do certain things. I think they believed in us, that we would do the right things. I think my parents felt, 'This is the way we want them to act. We expect them to act this way.' And we ended up acting that way." Louis McBurney says of his parents, "I don't remember many rules or regulations at all, just unspoken expectations. I knew I was expected to do well in school, to stay out of trouble. It was expected that I would do the right thing, and I did."

Communicating Expectations Through Your Own Actions

Good parents know that one of the best ways to communicate positive expectations of your children is through your own actions. "I had a lot of opportunities to get in trouble," remembers Judy Anderson, "but I could figure out my parents' expectations. And the kinds of things kids did to rebel, I didn't find relevant. Getting drunk, for example. I don't think my parents ever said to me, 'Don't drink.' But I didn't see them do it. I saw a lot of other people who did, and I knew who I wanted to be like. I wanted to be like my parents."

Giving Children the Gift of Trust

Perhaps because their expectations become a self-fulfilling prophecy, good parents trust their children a lot, and more often than not, their children live up to that trust. David Heim, for example, says that was true of his adolescence. "My parents trusted me a lot," he recalls. "Their trust was well founded. I knew what kind of life they expected me to lead, and on the whole, I agreed with it. I didn't have any interest in drinking beer, for example. I think my parents trusted me to some degree because I proved myself trustworthy, but I also didn't have many rebellious feelings toward them. So I didn't test the limits much."

Sometimes trusting your kids means trusting them not just to do the right thing but also to learn from their mistakes. "I think a lot about the prodigal son story," says David Handley. "Why in the world does the father let the son go into the far country when he knew he'd end up flat on his face? It took a lot of trust to let him go and let him make his own mistakes. That's what my parents did. They gave me the ability to make my own mistakes and learn from them."

The kind of trust that good parents have in their children is not blind trust. It is informed trust, trust not only in their children but also in the way they've raised their children. Some parents can't trust their children because they haven't raised them to be trustworthy. But more often than not, parents whose children don't want to disappoint them, who have taught their children how to make wise choices, who talk with and listen to their children, who have shown their children that actions have consequences, who have geared their discipline to their individual kids and their particular environment, who give reasons for their rules, who enforce their rules with love, reap the luxury of being able to give their children more and more freedom as they get older. And the more freedom children perceive, the less they seem to want to rebel.

That's what Keri Menconi realized as she reflected on the differences between her upbringing and that of her friend, who was constantly clashing with her harsh father. "I asked my dad once, 'Why weren't you a disciplinarian with us?'" Menconi recalls. "He made a fist with his hand and said, 'I look at it like this. When kids are younger, they are totally dependent on parents. But as they get older, we slowly open up our hands and let them go. When kids get into their teenage years, many parents tend to close the hand back up and try for more control. But I believe parents have to keep letting go gradually.'"

I suspect Menconi's father's analogy may be a key to why so many grown children of good parents talk about the tremendous sense of freedom they had growing up. It's unlikely they had total freedom as toddlers or as young grade-school children. My guess is that, consciously or unconsciously, their parents spent many years "loving them into direction"—and then gradually let go. Having gently guided them and expected them to do the right thing—having modeled how to do the right thing—they opened up their hands and trusted them to do the right thing.

· SIX ·

Make Your Children Proud of You

My mother was a very well-known singer in Rockford. I remember being in church when she would sing solos and feeling proud of her, proud that she was my mother.

Timothy Johnson

My dad was a great preacher. Among the Brethren, men were expected to preach, and he was always first class. He was always a very articulate person. When he spoke, he had a phenomenal memory. He had flaws, but I was even proud of his flaws.

Donald Cole

I was proud of my dad because I knew other people respected him, and he always stood up for what he believed in. He was my hero.

Nancy Swider-Peltz

AFTER SPENDING months puzzling over the widely varying styles of discipline described by adult children of good parents—and especially the almost total lack of overt discipline described by so many of those I interviewed—I began to realize that many of the parents I was hearing about didn't discipline their children for a very good reason: they didn't need to. They didn't need to because their children wanted to please them. But why do some children want to please their parents, when so many others would just as soon spite them?

I don't know all the reasons some children want to spite their parents. But I've come to the conclusion that many children of good parents want to please their parents because they admire and respect them because they're inordinately proud of them.

Take Madeleine L'Engle, for example. L'Engle grew up in a small apartment in New York City, the only daughter of an opera critic and a pianist. Many aspects of L'Engle's upbringing fly in the face of contemporary thinking about what makes for a healthy childhood: her parents disagreed "diametrically" on how to raise her. They were, according to L'Engle, very inconsistent in their childrearing techniques. They left her alone much of the time; she ate her meals alone in her room, for example, because it gave her time to read. But somehow, despite the fact that her parents quarreled over her, despite the fact that they seemed to be mystified as to how to raise a child, her parents managed to earn their daughter's undying admiration.

"My parents were people for whom I had great respect," L'Engle says. "They weren't 'Mommy and Daddy,' they were Mother and Father. They were people of integrity. They were honorable people. My mother always smelled lovely—I remember the fragrance she had—and my father was handsome and courteous and romantic. If I'd had any friends," she laughs, "I would have been proud to bring them home to meet my parents."

Then there's Nancy Swider-Peltz. Within a few minutes of meeting her, you become aware of several things. She's intense. She has strong convictions. And she's very proud of her parents—especially her father, a high-school physical-education teacher and coach, whom his daughter points to as the inspiration for her many athletic achievements.

"I've always felt I had something other people didn't have," Swider-Peltz says. "My dad was such a visible person in my life, and I looked up to him so much. He was a physical-education teacher, and he was what he preached. Very few parents were in the shape my dad was in. He was very strong. He made his own weights out of cement, and he kept himself looking so good. I remember him walking into my classroom sometimes when I was a little kid, and I would think, *He is the coolest dad!* And other people respected him for the same reasons.

"He was consistent in his classroom. He made kids feel good, even if he criticized or disciplined them. He was held in high respect because of his consistency and care. He was in control in his classes. He cared for his students and took time for them. People need boundaries, and he gave them. People respect a teacher like that.

"As a parent, he had great authority over us kids, but he also had a respect for us that I was always confident in. I felt my dad treated us so differently from the way other dads treated their kids. And I felt lucky my dad was like that. He gave us so much of his time and attention. We knew our dad wanted the best for us, and that made us look up to him."

Nancy Swider-Peltz admired her dad because she saw that others did, because he was competent and knowledgeable, and because of his vocational achievements. She even admired him because he was good looking. For these, and a variety of other reasons, Swider-Peltz and many other children of good parents seem to take unusual pride in their parents.

RESPECT FOR KNOWLEDGE
AND COMPETENCE

Children tend to respect their parents when they see them as knowledgeable and competent. Consider, for example, what these adult children remember about their parents.

"My dad has so many interests and is so bright," says Janet Getz. "He's a great teacher. Sometimes we'd come home and try to find things he didn't know. I really respect him for his intellect. Sometimes it's easier for me to talk about my mom, though. When we lived overseas, she wasn't able to get work permits, but she could do these wonderful things ministering to and caring for people. I really am proud of my parents and thankful to God for putting me in this family."

Like Getz, Jon Ebersole respects his father's intelligence and his mother's nurturing qualities. "My dad is a doctor and an extremely intelligent man," says Ebersole. "He knows quite a bit about a lot of things. He's extremely well-read, and he retains an amazing amount of what he reads. He can read a *National Geographic* and a year later carry on an intelligent conversation about what he read. My mom is a wonderful hostess and always filled our home with people."

Richard Chase respected his parents' business success because it reflected their competence in a wide range of areas. "My parents' dairy was doing fairly well after the end of the Depression and the beginning of the war," he recalls. "Things were going pretty well, so we knew our parents were pretty sharp, and we listened to them. If we wanted to know something, our parents generally knew it. My dad knew about horses, cattle, mechanical things, sports, even music. Everything I needed to know I simply learned from him. So I looked to him. Both my dad and mom were involved in business management. And Mom knew a lot. She kept the books for the dairy for a long time, and I helped her with the books and with doing some of the cooking and dishes and so forth. Mom taught piano and organ and had many students in and out constantly."

Gregg Roeber's pride in his father was rooted in the fact that his dad knew more than he did and could outperform him at many tasks. "The older I got," says Roeber, "the more it became obvious that my father was this tremendously important figure who ran this ranching operation that required a great deal of physical labor. He handled horses and cattle and dealt with all these physical sorts of things. As I began to work with him, I became quickly aware that I couldn't keep up with him. What's interesting is the fact that he took pains to laugh about it and say, 'This is exactly what my father told me when I started out.' He told me not to try to keep up with him, that it was a matter of getting used to it. 'I'm tougher, I'm older, it's not something to worry about.'"

RESPECT FOR ACCOMPLISHMENTS

Parents who know a lot and do a lot of things well tend to get things accomplished. And children take great pride in their parents' accomplishments. Kids are often very aware of their parents' career achievements, for example. Consider Ron Hutchcraft, who says he was inordinately proud of his father's success at work, which occurred against all odds. "My dad really improved himself in his job during my childhood and teenage years," says Hutchcraft. "Dad's mother died when he was four years old, and he had a tough economic situation in his family. When he graduated from high school, he had to go right to work. He worked very hard, right into the TB sanitarium. When he got into the business world, even though he didn't have a post-high-school education, he did have a tremendous love for people and therefore a great ability to work with them and win their trust. I remember when I was little, he was a machinist, and he used to come home in a rather beat-up jacket—he never really dressed up.

Then during my growing-up years, he became a foreman and then eventually a plant manager. And then I saw him always dressed up. He didn't travel that much, but when we'd take him to the airport, I used to think, *Boy, my father must really be important, because we have to take him to the airport, and he has a briefcase!*"

Joan Beck tells a similar story. "My father was a chemical engineer who worked his way up to become president and CEO of the town's largest industry, a company that made food products out of corn," she says. "At the time he was president, the company employed 1,500 people. My parents both worked their way through the University of Iowa at Ames, where they met. They were both the first people in their family to go to college. So I come from a very American-dreamish kind of family."

You Don't Have to Be a CEO

Fortunately, a parent doesn't have to be an executive at a large company to win his or her child's admiration. Gerhardt Jersild's parents had simple vocations—his father was a country pastor and his mother was a teacher—but they inspired great pride in their son. "My father came to the United States from Denmark because he wanted to become a Lutheran pastor," observes Jersild. "He didn't know any language except Danish, and there was no Danish seminary he could attend here. But he found a University of Denmark theologian who helped him get his theology education. My father was a very studious man. His English was not good, but he worked at it very hard, and it didn't keep people away from church. He was a really good preacher. Really a good man. My mother came here from Denmark after her mother told her, 'Anne, you can't stay here because you'll never be anything but a maid, and I don't want that.' So she was practically shoved onto the ship. She was seventeen years old and within a short time, she studied enough to pass the test to be a teacher. She was given a license to teach elementary school. My father was bright, but she was even brighter."

Benjamin Carson's mother spent much of her life working as a maid, but he was still extremely proud of her because of her incredible determination. "My mom had only a third-grade education," he observes, "but she spent a lot of time teaching herself to read. We'd often see her struggling to read the Bible—that's how she did it. Eventually she was successful and went on to get her GED. She then went to junior college and became an interior decorator."

PRIDE IN GOOD WORKS

Children are especially proud of their parents' accomplishments when they see the positive effect they have on other people. Brenda Watkins, for example, saw her father influencing some of the most important social issues affecting not only her community but the nation. "I was very, very proud of my dad," she muses. "I was in high school during the racial turmoil of the sixties, and it was exciting to me because my dad was so very involved. I remember when Ralph Abernathy spoke at my dad's church and when Martin Luther King died and my dad went to the funeral. There was this march, and for at least part of the way, my dad was one of the pallbearers. I remember him as being a very active kind of pastor, both in the black community and in San Francisco and in the outside community. I didn't always come out in the same place on some issues, but I appreciated that he was sensitive to some of the dynamics."

CREATING AN ATMOSPHERE OF RESPECT

Pride and respect are earned, not coerced. While parents obviously can't demand that their children be proud of them, they can create an atmosphere in which it's easy for their children to respect them by pointing out each other's accomplishments. David Handley, for example, recalls that his father was quick to sing his wife's praises. "My mom was Phi Beta Kappa in college and later a very successful French teacher," he says. "My dad respected her a great deal and always told me all about her academic accomplishments and about how beautiful she was. I think that affected my attitude toward women." It undoubtedly also affected his attitude toward his mother.

REFLECTED PRIDE

Children respect their parents when they see they are liked and respected by others. That was the case with Joan Beck. Her father was the CEO of the biggest industry in their town. Her mother was a leading community volunteer. They were, Beck recalls, exceptionally well thought of in the community.

"My father would occasionally take us down to the company where he worked," she says, "and everyone knew him by his nickname. His name was Roscoe Wagner, but everybody in town called him Wag. He knew everyone, absolutely everyone. I sensed they not only liked him but also respected him. He liked the guys who worked for him, and they liked him. It gave me a good feeling about him."

Jon Ebersole's parents were similarly well-known and liked in their small Ohio town, where his father was a prominent physician and his mother an acclaimed hostess. "My dad is very friendly, very outgoing," says Ebersole. "He has a politician's demeanor, although not a pompous kind of politician. He knew everyone in town, and everyone knew him. I think people in the community respected him. And Mom is very friendly. She's a wonderful hostess and is known throughout the extended family as well as the town as being a wonderful cook. I knew whenever I had friends over, she would make good food, and they would ooh and aah. That made me feel good."

Then there's David Heim, who grew up in a small New England town. Unlike some minister's kids, who seem to be embarrassed at being part of a clergy family, Heim says he was really proud of his parents, especially his father, because he was acutely aware of how others perceived them. "I saw the affection my dad created among the congregation," he explains, "and that reflected on us. We saw how other people thought the world of him. It was a small town, and my dad was there thirty years, so over time he had connections with nearly all the townspeople. He'd had a funeral for someone's relative, he'd served on a committee, stuff like that. So growing up, people would have good feelings about me because they knew my dad and had good feelings about him."

PEER PRIDE

Parents who want their children to be proud of them give their kids a reason to be proud of them in front of their friends. Person after person I interviewed told me how important it was to them that their parents related well to their friends, that they could introduce their parents to their peers without embarrassment. Take Nancy Tecson, for example. "I was always proud of my parents when my friends were over," she says. "I never felt embarrassed at all. I felt like, 'This is my mom!' I still feel that way. There's something about her. She's just real sweet, and she looks great, twenty years younger than she is. And my dad, too. I always felt very proud of my parents in front of my friends. I remember my friends would say, 'Oh, your dad is a really neat guy,' or, 'Your mom seems so nice.' It just makes me happy to be able to be proud of my parents like that."

Being Warm and Welcoming

Good parents are warm and welcoming to their children's friends. They take time to talk with them, as Jon Ebersole's parents did. "My dad, being a talker, always loved to meet my friends," says Ebersole. "My friends liked to call him 'Doc.' Both my parents were always interested in my friends. They were very cordial to them and encouraged me to have them over."

Showing Genuine Concern

When good parents talk to their kids' friends, they really listen. And, says Keri Menconi, they show genuine concern about the friends' lives, especially when they're adolescents. "I was proud of my parents because they were warm and accepting of my friends," says Menconi. "They were very hospitable, especially my mom. Two girls I've grown up with come from dysfunctional families, and it's been hard for them to come over to my house because I have the kind of family they want. But I definitely like bringing friends over because my parents will talk to them. My mom will ask how they're doing and genuinely care how their lives are going. Both my parents really care for people."

In part because of the concern her parents showed for her friends, Brenda Weaver's house became the acknowledged central meeting place for her high-school pals. "A lot of my friends felt comfortable coming over to talk to my dad even when I wasn't there," she explains. "One of my former boyfriends, for example, lost his father when he was ten, and I think my dad was a father figure for him. When we were breaking up, he would come over and see my dad and not me. My dad led a Bible study the summer after we graduated. We called it 'After Grads.' It was a once-a-week meeting where everyone could come, and my friends felt free to come and talk about things with my dad. They felt very at ease, especially around my dad. I've been told I'm so lucky to have parents like that to talk to. There's not another set of parents I would respect and admire more than my own. I felt that way throughout my adolescence, especially in high school. I know I'm so lucky. Sometimes I almost feel shy telling people because I'm afraid they won't believe me. I feel they'll think I'm exaggerating. I'm so lucky."

The Special Challenge of Adolescence

If there's ever a time when children are inclined not to be proud of their parents, it's adolescence. Teenagers seem to be embarrassed by the very fact of having parents. Even the most seemingly innocuous parental comment or action is capable of mortifying them. Wise parents know this, and prepare. They take the peer factor seriously, as O'Ann Steere's parents did. "My parents knew peers were a big thing," observes Steere. "They prayed from an early age about our adolescence, and they made our peers feel comfortable at our house—so much so that we came home from vacation once and some people from our youth group had let themselves in. They knew where the key was, and they were playing pool in the basement. I knew my parents wouldn't behave like jerks and embarrass me. I can remember other people being embarrassed of their parents, but I was never embarrassed of my parents."

PARENTS AS HEROES AND HEROINES

Parents who succeed in making their children proud of them give their kids a reason to see them as heroes and heroines. One of the best ways parents do that is by making a difference in the community. Something very powerful happens in the minds and hearts of kids when they see their parents devoting time and energy to altruistic causes. Listen to Kathy Beito talk about her parents, for example: "My parents are wonderful people," she says. "I wanted to be like them when I grew up. They were very involved in the community and helping other people. My mother was a Girl Scout leader, and we'd build a campfire in the woods and roast hot dogs. My friends used to think she did so many neat things. She was into reading and books and artwork. She started an art adventure program for young kids, and when friends came over to play, she had structured activities and projects we could do together. I remember she started a daycare center called Discovery Place. This pastor's wife would come over, and they'd have tons of meetings getting prepared for it. It's still a daycare center twenty years later. My dad was in the Rotary Club and involved in many sporting events in the community and money-raising things. I was proud of them, and I still am today. I look up to them and love to introduce them to people."

Like Kathy Beito's parents, good parents tend to be involved in their community. They're people who see needs and meet them. They're people who volunteer their time for good causes. They're people who see beyond themselves and their families.

"My parents were both pillar-of-the-community types," says Joan Beck. "My father was the kind of person who headed finance drives for the hospital and saw that the good causes worked. He was a financial trustee of the church and was on the board of trustees at the bank. He generally saw that the community was a viable place to live in. He made sure that what needed to be done *was* done.

"My mother worked in community organizations as a volunteer," Beck continues. "She was president of the YWCA for about six years. She organized a child-study group that's still in existence today. She volunteered at the hospital and did all the kinds of things that women volunteers did."

You Don't Have to Be a Star

After hearing so many stories like Beito's and Beck's, I began to wonder if you had to be a member of the local power elite to be a good parent! Not so. Consider pediatric neurosurgeon Benjamin Carson's mother or international evangelist Luis Palau's mom and dad, for example.

Abandoned by her husband, Carson's mother worked long hours as a maid to support her sons. But it never occurred to Carson or his brother to be ashamed of their mother because of her humble status in life. On the contrary, they took great pride in her tenacious, fighting spirit. "You just knew she wasn't going to take a lot of stuff from anybody," explains Carson, his voice full of admiration. "I remember when my brother was in junior high, the school wanted to put him into the curriculum for learning mechanics and things because in those days they didn't think a black kid would be going to college. My mother wouldn't hear of it. She went in and tore the place up. She said, 'My son is going to college!' And then there was the time we were in the car and this guy hit us. It was going to be a hit-and-run, but she got behind the wheel and chased that guy all through the city. Finally he just gave up. She got his insurance information and made him pay for the accident."

As evangelical Christians in an Argentinean society that looked down on Protestants, Luis Palau's parents were frequent targets of persecution. Their neighbors would stop in front of their house on religious holidays and perform a purifying ceremony that was understood to mean, 'These people are a blight on our community.' But Luis never shared the scorn of the surrounding community.

"My parents made me feel proud that I was a Palau," the evangelist recalls. "There was a pride of family, in the proper sense, even though we were considered heretics. I was proud of my father especially because he was a strong person, and people respected him as a businessman. I found out from conversations I would overhear that he would loan people money. Sometimes they couldn't pay after he had built them a house, and he would just let it go. The woman who lived across the street would always insult the family. One day she grabbed an electrical cable—the electricity was 220 and it could kill you—and she was screaming bloody murder. My dad, the man she insulted, ran over and saved her life. It changed the community. They were all talking about it, and I was very proud."

Not all parents can be community leaders. Not all parents have an opportunity to become heroes or heroines by saving someone's life. But most parents can find some way to make their children proud. Children seem to look for reasons to be proud of their parents, even if it's for a seemingly trivial reason like appearance. In fact, I've come to the conclusion that parents who downplay the importance of appearance may be missing an important opportunity to make their children proud of them.

Appearances Count to Kids

I was surprised, in conducting interviews with children of good parents, at how many people mentioned their great pride in the way their parents looked. I began to suspect that even children of good parents have been brainwashed by a world that places too much importance on physical beauty and outward appearance. But even my oldest interview subject, Gerhardt Jersild, a retired attorney in his eighties, mentioned his Danish immigrant father's appearance as a point of pride. "I was proud of my father," Jersild told me. "He was a tall fellow. Straight. He always wore his derby or a straw hat in the summer. And he always wore a black suit." Jersild's pride in his minister father's dignified black suit and appropriately seasonal hat reflected similar feelings on the part of many others I talked to. Judy Anderson says of her parents, "People have this concept of missionaries as these dowdy fuddyduddies. But my parents weren't like that. They always dressed normally. They always looked good." Molly Cline comments, "My parents are a very handsome couple. They're slender, very well groomed, very attractive. People will say, 'I can't believe they're your parents!' and that makes me feel very proud." Donald Cole says, "We were always proud to introduce our parents. My dad always looked as if he'd stepped out of a department-store window. He was a good-looking man and a natty dresser. He was tall, over six feet. I respected my dad."

Children want to be proud of their parents. Good parents give their children reasons to respect, admire, and be proud of them. They develop areas in which they are knowledgeable and competent. They accomplish things by combining their knowledge and expertise with hard work. They become heroes and heroines in their children's eyes by giving their time and energy to altruistic causes. They are warm and welcoming and accepting of their children's friends. They don't overlook the importance of personal appearance.

Having said all this, don't be discouraged if you're not president of a company or head of most of the charities in town or a beauty queen. I'm convinced that you don't have to be an overachiever who looks like a film star to be a good parent. I'm convinced of that in part because of the reflections of Dick Martens, an attorney and involved father, who had this to say about his own parents: "Neither of my parents made a gigantic mark on the world, but that didn't mean as much as their investment and care toward me as a kid. I was proud of them because they were good parents. All the Nobel prizes in the world aren't going to make up for what I got as a child. The world may see it one way, but a kid sees it another."

If there's anything I've learned from talking to children of good parents, it's this: Dick Martens is right. The world may see things one way, but kids see it another.

·SEVEN·

Create Community

It's a tremendous feeling to be connected to a number of people who know you and love you and care about you. It's a tremendous strength.

Judy Anderson

"IT TAKES A VILLAGE to raise a child." I've been impressed by the wisdom of this African proverb ever since I first heard it quoted. I think the truth of it was well articulated in a column titled, "A tribal solution to family woes," by William Raspberry of the *Washington Post*. Raspberry quoted a former Xerox executive and "committed family man" as saying, "The problem with today's children is that the tribe is no longer functioning."

The tribe?

Raspberry described "the tribe" as a village with four important elements: the core family, the wider community, the political leadership, and the religious leadership. The unwritten covenant of the tribe, he says, is that all four elements are responsible for bringing children to responsible adulthood.

After talking with scores of people who appreciated their parents and who grew up to become well-adjusted, productive adults, I've come to believe it's true. It takes a village of caring friends, relatives, and acquaintances—people who to a large degree share your most deeply held values—to raise children who adopt those values, who grow up with a strong sense of security, and who develop strengths beyond those you alone could give them.

Good parents inherently understand this. Consciously or unconsciously, they make it possible for their children to become part of a community, a community that is larger than their nuclear family. To the greatest extent possible in their particular circumstances, they participate as active members of an extended family. They develop deep friendships and expose their children to their friends. They are hospitable. They open their homes to relatives, business acquaintances, people in need, and individuals who have potential to be heroes and heroines in their children's eyes.

EXTENDED FAMILY LIFE

Repeatedly, children of good parents spoke to me about warm memories of participation in a close-knit extended family. Richard Chase remembers with delight what it was like growing up on the same California ranch with his cousins and their parents. Grace Ketterman recalls life on a farm with an aunt who always came to stay when a baby was born or when someone was sick and an uncle who was always around to help. She remembers huge clan events where the extended family would get together to butcher pork or beef and then cook the meats in enormous outdoor pots. Louis McBurney reminisces about a childhood spent basking in the love and approval of not only his mother but also the grandmother and aunt with whom they lived in a sleepy southern town while his father was off fighting in World War II. McBurney relishes mental pictures of his mother and aunt at the piano, of big spreads of food laid out by his grandmother—homemade ice cream, fried squash, fried okra, fried chicken—lots of music and laughter and games. Hot summer days, hot summer nights. Running barefoot, being carefree.

Sometimes, participation in extended family life is an accident of geography. But good parents tend to be very intentional about arranging their lives in ways that provide an active community of family members for their children. Terry Tochihara, for example, who grew up in a tight-knit Japanese-American family, says her parents made a very conscious choice to live in proximity to relatives and recalls at least one extended family function every week of her childhood.

As the son of Norwegian immigrants, Lowell Olberg's ethnic heritage is very different from Tochihara, but his sense of connectedness within a family network is very similar. "Family—the immediate family and the cousins, aunts, and uncles—was the nucleus of our life," recalls Olberg. "My mother's family was all in the area, while none of my dad's family lived nearby. Yet my dad went along with my mother's family as much as if it were his own. And over the years it was his family. We tended to visit cousins every couple of weeks."

Obviously, close geographical proximity makes it easier to nurture extended family relationships. But many good parents make an effort to maintain extended family relationships even when it isn't convenient. Like Kathy Beito's parents, they will travel for hours several times a year to go see the grandparents. And they come up with creative solutions to problems of distance. When Don Cole's extended family began scattering across the country, for example, they didn't let the miles keep them apart; they just gathered up all the aunts and uncles and cousins and took their vacations together.

The Gift of Grandparents

Good parents, if possible, give their children the gift of a close relationship with grandparents. Often, grandparents can be resources to children in ways that parents can't. They frequently have more time to be emotionally and even physically available to a child. And they can provide experiences unique to their own lives and personal histories. Wise parents recognize this without resentment and not only allow their children to develop a special relationship with grandparents but also encourage it, as Jody Hedberg's mother did. "Even though I was her only child," recalls Hedberg, "my mother encouraged my relationship with my grandmother. My grandmother Hobbs didn't have any daughters, only sons, so for that reason, my mother was willing to share me. And my grandmother was a very strong influence on my life. I adored her. I spent summers with her, and she was a real role model."

Parents who encourage their children to develop a relationship with grandparents give their kids a gift of extra love and wider experience. "My father's mother was a very warm, outgoing, extraordinarily affectionate person," remembers Dick Martens. "That added a lot to my development. My mother's mother was a much more worldly person. She worked basically all her adult life, and she traveled, bringing other dimensions to us as kids. She would take us to downtown Chicago sometimes, and we'd ride the 'el' and go to restaurants. Those were exciting times for small children. It was nice."

Many grown children of good parents grew up with a live-in grandparent in their home, and they tend to see this as a great benefit. Elaine Kirk, for example, had her paternal grandparents live with her family on the farm. "My dad bought a little house for them," she recalls, "and put it in our backyard. When my grandmother died, my grandfather stayed on. He would fix his own breakfast, but my mother would bring him lunch and invite him to join us for dinner at night. Mother cared for him, took care of all his laundry, and that sort of thing. We all just adored him."

What children observe about how their parents treat live-in grandparents teaches them a lot more about respecting their elders than any lecture ever could. Jay Kesler comments, "My father's father lived with us until I was about eight years old. I observed my dad with his dad, which was interesting. Both were strong Germanic people, but I watched my dad's deference to his own dad. This honor-your-father-and-mother stuff was modeled as well as talked about. My dad really took care of his aging father, and I never heard him or my mother complain about that."

Parents can't always be available every time a child needs someone to listen and understand, but a live-in grandparent can often fill in the gaps. Grace Ketterman says that was very true of her live-in grandmother. "She was an extremely important person in my life in a quiet way," says Ketterman. "She was a very peaceful, wonderful person. She was deaf, but she could talk. Whenever I was upset, I could go to her and cry. She never criticized me or anyone else. She just let me cry. She was a beautiful influence on me."

Non-parent Parents

In addition to grandparents, other relatives can be important resources in a child's life. These relatives can be unabashed cheerleaders, perhaps because they don't see the behavior of someone else's child as a reflection on themselves and perhaps because they have no responsibility for discipline. That's how Louis McBurney remembers his beloved Aunt Lottie. "Everyone should have an Aunt Lottie in their lives," he says. "She thought I was the best thing that ever happened to humanity. She worked in a department store in Waco, and she would take me in and show me off to people. She just generally spoiled me terribly."

Author and teacher O'Ann Steere says much of what she is today stems from the influence of her own remarkable aunt, who continues to be a positive presence in her life. "Two years ago," she says, "I was installed as president of Covenant Women in a five-state area. We're talking about a five-minute deal—you walk up to the platform, they lay hands on you, and you're done. My aunt showed up from Moline to see me prayed for. A three-hour drive for a five-minute prayer! But she showed up. She was not only there theoretically, but her body was there."

Beloved relatives can also fill in the occasional gaps that occur in a parent-child relationship as Mary O'Connor recalls: "On my mother's side, I had an aunt who was also my godmother, and she was really good to me. I always felt if I wasn't getting along with my mom, I could talk to her or write to her. She was my friend."

THE NEIGHBORHOOD NETWORK

Good parents know that community doesn't just happen inside families. Often, friends, neighbors, fellow church members, and even business colleagues can provide the sense of connectedness and rootedness that can be so important in giving children a feeling of safety and security. Joan Beck, for example, recalls some neighbors who became like extended family members for her and her sister. "We called this couple who lived on our block 'Aunt' and 'Uncle,' and we remained close to them as children. We'd go on picnics together and share many family activities."

Mary Kay Ash wouldn't have had much of a family life at all if it hadn't been for some of her neighbors, who became her adopted parents and siblings. Ash's mother, who was forced to work long hours to support her daughter and invalid husband, gratefully encouraged her little girl to spend time with her neighborhood friends and their families. As a result, Ash developed a special friendship with a little girl named Dorothy, who lived around the corner. "Dorothy was my extended family," recalls Ash. "I'd go to her house and walk to school with her. She was a tiny, thin little child who never wanted to eat. Her mother would give her this beautiful toast with strawberry jam on it and milk with ice in it—I still drink milk with ice today—but Dorothy would say she wasn't hungry, so I would eat it. I ate her breakfast every day. I also went on vacations with their family and participated in their Christmas activities and Easter egg hunts. My parents thought it was wonderful that I had an opportunity to be with Dorothy. Her mother was so nice to me. She treated me like her own child, and that was very helpful to me."

CREATING COMMUNITY THROUGH HOSPITALITY

Good parents create community by extending hospitality. They open their homes to relatives, friends, acquaintances—people who not only benefit from their hospitality, but who by their very presence expanded the horizons of their hosts' children.

Luis Palau says hospitality was important in his parents' house. It seemed to him that they were always inviting relatives and missionaries and visiting preachers over for meals and overnight stays. "People were always coming and going," he recalls. "There was a lot of bustle. As I look back, it seemed natural. My parents used to quote the verse in Hebrews about practicing hospitality because you may be entertaining angels unaware."

Madeleine L'Engle remembers her pianist mother and opera-critic father opening their New York apartment to friends every Sunday night during opera season. "We had an open house every Sunday night for the first twelve years of my life," she recalls. "We never knew how many people were going to come—anywhere from half a dozen to twenty-five. The stars of the Met would come over, and while my mother played the scores of operas, they would sing. So that was a very rich background. Although I was in my bedroom and wasn't part of it, I still absorbed a love of music. Probably the best thing of all was the feeling that art is good. Some kids grow up being taught that art is bad, if not wicked. I grew up being taught that art is wonderful. I have always looked at art as a way of glorifying God."

Former radio-program host Melinda Schmidt credits her hospitable parents with giving her a worldview that extended beyond the bounds of their middle-class suburb: "My family practiced active hospitality," she says. "We always had company. My dad was very involved in the church missions committee, so we always had missionaries from the missions conference at our home. That was great exposure. Plus my dad was in international work, and he would have customers in our home, which was great. It gave us another perspective. I remember we had a lot of people from Asia, South America, and Italy. I think it was just wonderful. It showed us the world was bigger than our hometown. We learned about other cultures and developed great friendships. One man from Taiwan is like part of our family. I loved the exposure to all these different people. It really broadened our world."

Parents who don't have international business contacts—in other words, most parents—can still create powerful learning opportunities for their children by inviting visiting missionaries or foreign students to share a meal or stay overnight. Grace Ketterman is one of many adult children who say that their parents' hospitality to people of many backgrounds and cultures greatly enriched their lives. "Missionaries were often guests in our home," recalls Ketterman. "To get to know a

Chinese pastor or nationals from Nigeria or other exotic places—these were fairy tales to me as a child!"

Even less exotic hospitality makes a positive impression on children. Jay Kesler grew up in a small town and didn't get to meet many foreign visitors, but he believes he's benefited tremendously from the example of his parents' hospitality to other family members. Sometimes showing hospitality is hardest when it's the relatives who are the guests. Especially when they're frequent guests. "I had an aunt and uncle who showed up five out of six Sundays," explains Kesler. "They lived in the country. They would go to church, stay in town, and come to our house for Sunday dinner. My mother finally caught on and planned on it, but it was never announced. Every Sunday we played with the same cousins. They ate the same chicken we did. As children we loved it. I've watched my mother do this with many relatives—people who were down on their luck or having trouble. I think our home was known for that."

Steve Roskam's home was known for hospitality too, and like other children of good parents, he appreciated it. "My parents would always open up their house to other people," he says. "I remember having all kinds of foreign graduate students coming over. To this day, my parents have people staying with them. Ever since I can remember, the door has always been open. You never really had to ask if you could bring your friends over. I'd come home from college with three people and say, 'Hi, Mom, these are my friends.' I always knew my friends were welcome. We even had one of my friends from high school live with us. His parents moved, and he wanted to finish his senior year, so they said, 'Oh, come stay with us.' There was a constant stream of people through there."

A COMMUNITY OF FRIENDS

A surprisingly important factor in the lives of grown children of good parents is their parents' network of friends. Good parents tend to have strong friendships, friendships that span many years. Timothy Johnson recalls that his parents had a large network of friends—both individually and together. "My father was active in a group of men who called themselves the Highland Securities," he says. "It started out as a social group to buy stocks together. That quickly went by the boards, but they remained close friends for the rest of their lives and got together once a month. I can remember many times when the men gathered and the kids were around and got to know them. My mother was very active in the Mary Martha Circle at church, and they too would be in our home. Each had a social club or circle."

Attorney Dick Martens tells a similar story: "My parents had lots of friends. To this day they do a lot of entertaining. What's interesting is that they have friends who go all the way back to high school. My mother is seventy-five, and she's still getting together with this group called the 'Biscuit Babes,' who are her high-school chums. I'm impressed by the fact that she was able to keep those relationships, and my father is the same way."

Keri Menconi is still young—just out of college—but she's already had time to reflect on the importance of her parents' friends during her growing-up years. "My parents had these friends, Jack and Kathy, who would take us out a lot when we were younger," she says. "They'd take us bowling or to an amusement park and stuff like that. That was nice. They were adults who shared our parents' values and were a good example, but they weren't our parents."

It's the very fact that your parents' friends aren't your parents—and still share their values—that's so important, says Jay Kesler. "Three men my dad worked with in the factory were probably closer to me than uncles," he says. "These were affinity friendships that developed out of working together. They also spent most of their weekends together—fishing, helping with chores, fixing cars together. They were very close friendships. Their wives were like second mothers to me. I was convinced they would take care of me if something happened to my parents. That made me feel very stable.

"I see these kinds of friendships as missing in young people's lives today," he continues. "The isolation of not having your parents' friends around to help communicate values—sexual information, for example—is not healthy. I think it's largely a myth that parents are able to communicate sexual information. However, a favorite uncle or a fishing buddy can communicate these things to a boy. If the friend and the father are in tune, the friend's communication becomes the same as the parents', only more effective. I'm not sure kids' ears are able to hear their parents on these subjects. It may also be true of other subjects. Kids know what their parents feel, but they want to test it against other people. If they can test them with their parents' friends, they may not have to test them with other people who hold totally different values."

It should be noted that kids can't benefit much from their parents' friends if their parents don't include them, at least some of the time, in their social life. By including their children in appropriate aspects of their adult world, good parents allow their children to "overhear" adult conversations and develop a context for understanding their parents' values.

INSTITUTIONAL VILLAGES

Even institutions can create a village backdrop for raising a child. Fred Barnes grew up in suburban Washington D.C., where he says there was very little sense of rootedness or geographic community. But his family was part of a strong military tradition—his father, maternal grandfather, and uncle all graduated from West Point. "Many of my parents' friends were in some way connected to West Point," Barnes recalls. "That was sort of their community. They were a homogeneous group. They all pretty much thought alike in terms of spiritual, political, and social values. So my parents' friends probably reinforced their values."

The Church as a Village

The church is one of the most common institutional villages in which children of good parents grow up. Harold Best, for example, recalls a childhood spent moving from one pastorate to another. Because of his parents' frequent moves, long-term friendships were next to impossible. But in each new town, he says, the church served as a familiar community. Many other children of good parents, whether they lived in one community their whole lives or moved frequently like Harold, spoke of parents who made sure that the church was part of their communal village.

The current emphasis on reclaiming "family values" hasn't sufficiently defined what "family" means. The kind of family children need in order to grow up healthy is more than the nuclear family—although an intact nuclear family is certainly desirable. The fact is, children benefit tremendously from another kind of family values: immersion in extended family life. Close relationships with grandparents, non-parent parents, neighbors, and even business colleagues. Strong friendships. Hospitality. Affiliation with institutions made up of people who share your strongly held convictions.

These are some of the components of life in a village. And as good parents know, it takes a village to raise a child.

◆ EIGHT ◆

Make Your Children Feel Safe

I always had the feeling that my parents were a safety net. That I could take risks I might not have otherwise. I knew I wouldn't crash. Not that I ever really needed it. But it was a good feeling to know they were always there.

Joan Beck

We'd come home and mother was always there. I have so many memories of coming in on a bitter winter day after ice skating, and mother would always have hot cookies, stuff like that.

Donald Cole

Most subjects were okay to talk about with my parents. We could always tell them how we felt.

Keri Menconi

PHARAOH HAD DECREED that all male children born to his Hebrew slaves were to be put to death. So a young Hebrew mother put her infant son in a basket and hid him in a marsh, where she prayed he would be found by an Egyptian princess.

126

In so doing, she gave up her dreams of raising him, loving him, encouraging him, nurturing his spiritual values, laughing with him, guiding him. Her first priority was to keep her little boy safe.

One of the foundational responsibilities of parenthood is assuring the safety of our children. Children have an innate need to know they are safe. They look to their parents to protect them, to make them feel secure. And while it is impossible in a flawed and broken world to shield our children from all hurt and harm and danger, good parents raise their children in ways that assure them of at least one place they can always go—and be safe.

Parents can't always guarantee physical safety. Jewish parents in Hitler's Germany couldn't protect their children from the concentration camp. Somalian parents today can't protect their babies from slow starvation. But safety is more than physical. Physical safety is the most basic, but emotional safety is equally—perhaps more—important.

PHYSICAL SAFETY

Keeping your kids safe from physical harm seems like a fairly basic concept. But in an era of rampant child abuse and neglect, it's worth mentioning that good parents care about the physical safety of their kids.

Dick Chase recalls that, while his parents rarely raised their voices, they did when the threat of danger was imminent. "When Dad was really loud or shouting, it was usually because we were messing around with equipment or machinery or with horses, and we were getting too smart," he says. "I have one memory of five or six of us on one horse, riding bareback. At times we'd do something that could be pretty dangerous, and I remember him shouting, 'Stop! Get off!' And I remember one time crawling up in a silo when we probably could have broken a leg or arm, and we got whaled on that time. Raised voices and physical punishment were rarities except where they were related to danger."

The relative freedom described by children of good parents was limited by the bounds of potential physical harm. Nancy Tecson comments, "The only thing my dad would keep my sister and me from was something that might be dangerous, like mowing the lawn. He'd never let us do that. He was afraid we'd cut our hands." Gregg Roeber reflects, "One of the few times I can remember getting a spanking was during the summer. Near our house were stock ponds in which we were not allowed to go swimming because there were no guards or adults around to take care of us. One of my friends came over and pestered me and insisted on swimming in the ponds. I finally gave in. Both of us got a thorough talking to and thrashing."

Discerning When to Protect

While it's not possible or even desirable to protect children from all pain, disappointment, or failure, good parents try to protect their kids from irreversible harm—or overwhelming odds.

Dr. Benjamin Carson doesn't remember ever feeling afraid in the ghetto where he lived with his mother and brother because he was convinced his mother could handle anything and everything that might come along. Carson laughingly recalls, "I felt as safe with my mother there as I would have with a father in the house because my mother wasn't afraid of anything. If some big burly burglars came in, shame on 'em. They were in big trouble!"

Donald Cole has never forgotten the time his father, a no-nonsense bank executive and former Marine, rescued him from peril at the hands of an enraged neighbor. Cole had just gotten his driver's license—he was only fourteen, but in those days you could drive at that age—and he was using his father's car to practice. "One day," Cole recalls, "I scraped some guy's car as I was coming down the alley. He didn't leave room, and I didn't have enough experience to know I couldn't make it. So I pulled up to our house, put the car in the garage, and this guy was in pursuit. He was yelling and shouting at me. Dad came out of the house and said, 'Go into the house. I'll take care of this.' The next thing I saw was this guy tearing down the alley with my dad after him. When my dad came back, he never mentioned a thing at all. Never mentioned the car, just got it fixed. My pursuer was an older guy, and I was a kid. The odds weren't even. So my dad evened them!"

EMOTIONAL SAFETY

Emotional safety underlies some of the dominant characteristics of good parents. Unconditional love makes kids feel safe, as does consistent discipline, a sense of community, a positive atmosphere, spiritual values, and parents who love each other.

But other, more specific characteristics of good parents also contribute to a sense of emotional safety and security: good parents tend to create families rich in ritual and tradition. They make it safe for their kids to talk, to disagree, and even to fail. And they allow their children to change and grow.

Ritual and Tradition

"We live by structure," observes Madeleine L'Engle. "Without structure, we're not even human. We're gangs." L'Engle points to an important principle: like almost any other unit of society, families need structure. They should be flexible, yes, but structured at the same time. Sort of like a human body. Thanks to the structure of the human skeleton, we can bend, stretch, run. Without our skeletons, we would be little more than enormous multi-cellular amoebas.

Rituals and traditions are the skeletons of family life. They provide the structure that makes children feel secure. The power of routine in everyday life, for example, is grossly underestimated. Children of good parents say routine was the thread that held together the fabric of their lives. Take the Martens. "Our family was very ritualized," says Dick Martens. "Everything had a strong rhythm to it in terms of when my father would wake us up in the morning, when my mother would prepare breakfast or lunch. When we started going to school, my father would frequently drop us off at the bus stop and go to work. We would go with my mother when she went shopping for groceries. My father would be home every night by 5:30 or 6:00, and we always had dinner at 6:15. I think it's important for kids to have a sense of security and predictability about how things are going to be handled and where they're going to go. We had an extraordinary predictability."

Mealtimes provide an opportunity for routines that compute positively to children. Kathy Beito remembers the comfortable knowledge that the whole family would be together—and certain rituals would be observed—at meals. "Breakfast and dinner were very ritualized at our house," she says. "I knew we would all eat breakfast together. I'd go to catch the bus to go to school, and Dad would go off to work. It was expected that we eat dinner together. We always had devotions and said the 'Come Lord Jesus' prayer before each meal."

Lowell Olberg reminisces about the certainty of coffee and conversation after certain meals. "We had a big meal at noon, and then we would sit afterward and drink coffee for an hour or so, especially if we had guests or if it was after church on Sunday," he recalls. "The only reason we'd leave the table was so they could clean it up to have afternoon coffee, and then we'd sit down and have more coffee."

Andy Tiebert laughingly reflects on the predictability of the menu options during his childhood: "I thought everybody ate scrambled eggs on Saturday, cereal on Sunday, and poached eggs on Wednesday. We still eat lasagna at Christmas because that's my sister's birthday, and we always got our favorite meal on our birthday."

Holiday Traditions

Establishing family holiday traditions is another wonderful way to make kids feel safe. Children find comfort in eating the same dishes every Thanksgiving, going to the same relatives' houses every Christmas, coloring eggs in the same way every Easter. It doesn't seem to matter which holiday is emphasized or what rituals you use to observe it, but creating a fuss and doing it over and over the same way each year makes a big impression on kids.

Gerald Koenig says some of his most vivid memories from childhood center on Christmas. "I remember the whole family in the car on the way to the Christmas Eve service and singing Christmas carols as we traveled the seven miles to the church. One room in our house would be blocked off for the Christmas tree. No one would be allowed to go into the parlor for a couple of days before Christmas. My parents would put the Christmas tree up the night before, and then we would have our Christmas Eve service. We'd go to the worship service and come home and then we would line up by age, the youngest to the oldest, to enter this room. My parents would open the door, and we would walk in to find our gifts on the sofa. Each of us would have a stack. We'd open those gifts and then we would stay dressed up for worship because we went back to the midnight service. We'd ride back to church and again sing carols. We usually wouldn't sing on the way back because the younger ones were falling asleep by that time. And the next day we would go to the grandparents for Christmas celebration. That was absolute and occurred every year."

Both Christmas and Thanksgiving were laden with tradition at Mary O'Connor's house. "I could write a book about the things we did at Christmas," she enthuses. "We always invited our childless neighbors for breakfast. We cut down the tree together and had cookies with the people who owned the pine forest. We put the tree up on a certain day before Christmas, and then our parents wouldn't let us in the living room. We ate that stuff up. For Thanksgiving, we'd go to my grandfather's house. He was an old man, and my mother would bring everything. All the families in the area would meet there. We did that for years and years."

Children love it when they can count on the same foods, the same relatives, and the same stories at every family holiday. That's the way it was in Timothy Johnson's family. "Our holiday gatherings happened like clockwork," he explains. "We would have a huge meal with all the trimmings. Uncle Joe was always the one who carved the turkey, and then we would all tell the same old family stories around the table."

Not all families have a strong ethnic identity, but those who do can mark the holidays in children's minds with special ethnic holiday traditions. Kathy Beito comments, "We always celebrated Christmas with Norwegian delicacies and Norwegian flags on the tree. I really have fond memories of that and Thanksgiving, with the traditional roll to get our stomachs stretched out. We'd all be rolling around on the floor."

Holiday traditions don't just happen on their own. Somebody needs to make them happen. On a practical level, it often helps if one parent takes on the responsibility for creating and orchestrating the many little rituals that become family traditions. O'Ann Steere, for example, says holiday traditions were a hallmark of her family life mainly because of her mother. "You name a holiday, and we had a tradition," she says. "Billions. My mother initiated them, and my dad was snappy enough to realize that he was not good in this area. He had specifically delegated that to my mother before they ever had children. He said, 'This is one of the things I love about you and hope you'll be able to teach me and make part of our family.'"

Family-oriented holiday traditions do more than create memories. As Mary O'Connor points out, they also create a very real bond between the family members who observe them. "I was one of thirteen grandchildren," she says, "and even though we live all over the country now, we don't feel separate from each other. There's a real bond there, a feeling we're not alone in the world."

Dependability

Good parents make their children feel safe because they are dependable. They keep their promises. They are predictable. And they're there when their kids need them. Take Nancy Tecson's dad, for example. "My dad has always been just like a rock," she says. "Absolutely dependable. When we were kids, he was a salesman. That meant he was around. His hours were flexible. He'd leave late and come back early. Because of the job he had, he was available to take us places. If there was a medical emergency or something, my dad was the one who would bring us to the doctor. He was the person we all fell back on when something was really wrong. I remember when I was about two, I'd wake up in the middle of the night sometimes, and I couldn't go back to sleep. So I'd go to my parents' room and tap my dad on the shoulder. He'd look at me—I'd be at eye level—and he'd get up and follow me and get in my bed with me. That kind of stuff. My dad was a big, solid, trustworthy, rock type of person. We could always depend on him."

Safe to Talk

Good parents make it safe for their kids to talk to them. They let their kids have opinions and feelings, even if they disagree with the opinions and wish the feelings were different. They don't give up their own principles, but they're slow to judgment. They're inclined to listen rather than lecture.

Brenda Weaver remembers, "I never felt afraid to go to my parents with anything. They never made me feel ashamed. They made sure I wasn't afraid to bring something up to them. I could ask for help, and they were always interested. In my high-school and college years, I could tell them about things my friends would never tell their parents. I never had secrets from them."

Doug Anderson says his mother made him feel it was safe to talk to her by resisting the temptation to jump to conclusions or to condemn. "If there was something I ever wanted to tell my mother," Anderson says, "I always could. She had advice, but she never came down as judgmental. She'd hold judgment in her mind. She listened. She was very good at listening."

Good parents know that listening isn't, or at least shouldn't be, a conditional act. They don't stop listening just because they don't agree with the opinions their children are expressing. "I wasn't always right," observes O'Ann Steere, "but my parents always let me have my say. I never felt, 'They won't even shut up and listen.' When I wanted to go out on Halloween when I was eight, when I wanted to go parasailing as a teenager, they always listened."

Children don't feel free to talk unless they know their parents are really listening. Since it's often difficult to drop everything and give kids the kind of undivided attention that makes them feel they're being heard, some parents set aside a special "listening" time. In Brenda Weaver's family, dinnertime was the time to listen to each other. "We had this thing called 'good thing/bad thing,'" she explains. "We'd tell the good and bad things that happened during the day, and we always heard each other."

Nancy Gruben's mother reserved a special listening time at the end of each day. "She gave me five minutes of uninterrupted time right before I went to bed," Gruben recalls. "It went on until I was about thirteen or fourteen. She called it 'Nancy time.' I could talk about anything I wanted to. It was a really nice time of day. Five minutes to talk to her about anything."

Kids want more than time, of course. They want their parents' focused attention. One way parents can focus their attention—and show their children they're actively listening—is to ask appropriate questions. Judy Anderson: "My parents are really good people to bounce ideas off of. They'll raise questions: Have you thought about this? Have you considered this? They don't have preconceived ideas, and if they do, I can fight with them on it. They're very open."

Of course, the risk for parents in opening themselves to a nonjudgmental listening stance is the possibility that their children will confide in them about activities they feel are wrong, about actions that require consequences. In such instances, wise parents resist the temptation to deliver an angry lecture or heap on blame. Instead, they calmly outline the consequences and make sure they follow through. For instance, take what David Heim's mother did the time he confessed to playing hooky from school. "My friend and I went hiking," he explains. "We didn't do it very shrewdly because we showed up at school and then left, so I knew I was going to have trouble the next day. But I remember clearly explaining to my mom what I'd done and why I thought I had to do it. I was tired of school . . . it was such a nice day. . . . It turned out to be a rather pleasant conversation. My mom really wasn't very censuring about it. She just laid out what we were going to have to do: Go to school the next day and talk to the principal the first thing." Confessing to the principal was a sufficiently unpleasant consequence to deter further truancy, and in enforcing that consequence without verbal condemnation, Heim's mother wisely kept open the lines of communication with her son.

Good parents are confident enough in their belief system and in the values they've given their children that they aren't afraid to listen to new ideas. "If I came home with new and different ideas, especially from college," reflects Gretchen Ziegenhals, "my parents were always open to what I had to say. They weren't so rigid that they couldn't listen. They didn't necessarily agree with me, but I never felt I was going to burst the family bubble if I had a new idea. They would say, 'Well, do you have something we could read about this?' I remember when I first discovered feminism and decided that was just a great idea, they weren't totally thrilled, but they were interested and open and listened. I remember when I came home and announced to my mother that, much to her disappointment, God is not a father. God is not a man! And my mother wanted to hear more about that. I knew that wasn't up her alley, I knew she disagreed, but she was interested because she wanted to know where my thoughts were and what I was going through, what I was thinking.

"I remember her coming to visit me at seminary. She spent the weekend, and we had a lot of fun. I took her all around. After spending the weekend together, I was putting her in a cab to go back to the airport and she was trying to think of all the last-minute things she wanted to say to me, and she said, 'Oh, by the way, oh, I know. . . . How's your feminism coming?' It was so transparent! But it was her way of saying, 'I want to affirm you. I want to be interested, even though I'm not sure what this is all about.' But it was so funny!

"One time we took a train ride to my aunt's house, just my mom and me, and we were talking about feminist theology and she said, 'Well, you know, I am really quite comfortable with the idea of God as a father and that brings me a lot of comfort and I like that. So I think I'll just stick with that.' And that was okay with both of us. We knew we didn't agree there, but I knew where she was coming from and she knew where I was coming from. So I'm not afraid to state opinions that I know they would disagree with. I know they're open to listening and talking."

Good parents are open to a healthy airing of issues, even if things get a bit loud. To look at Julie Ravencroft, a demure-looking blonde in her early thirties, you'd never suspect her of rabble-rousing. But she freely admits being one of a whole family of soap-box orators. "My dad was captain of the debate team in school and has raised a bunch of kids who are all really good at debating," she explains. "We get into really loud, heated discussions. That's where our obstinate, opinionated, German blood comes out. It can get really loud, but at the same time, it's neat. We all are able to let go and express our opinions. It's never acrimonious. It can be frustrating when you feel strongly about something and others disagree, but there's real permission in our family to have individual views and attitudes."

Good parents don't just tolerate animated discussion, they encourage it. Brenda Watkins says some of her favorite memories of growing up are related to "rousing discussions" she used to have with her dad and brothers. "My dad was very engaging," she says. "He had an ability to pull us into conversation. He encouraged our own articulation of views. That's helped me a lot. It's validated me in so many ways. I had the right, and I was encouraged to have an opinion. That's good and important. It was a very accepting environment for the most part. A few times I felt I wasn't heard, but I felt as if I grew up with parents who wanted the best for me and who would support me."

Safe to Rebel

Fred Barnes went through some rough years with his parents. Or perhaps it would be more accurate to say that his parents went through some rough years with him. It started in high school, when he got caught cheating on an exam and was suspended from his private prep school. Naturally, his parents were crushed and terribly hurt. Then after high school, Barnes decided not to take his appointment to West Point, where his father, uncle, and grandfather had all gone. He did go into the army, though, after a year in junior college, and when he came back home, the tensions between Barnes and his parents widened into a gulf.

"It was a pretty rocky period," Barnes, now a respected Washington journalist, recalls. "They complained about my lifestyle. They thought my hair was too long, that I stayed out too long, that I drank too much. They were right, and we had some fights. I remember one time we got into a fight because my parents thought I needed a haircut. I probably did. But I stormed out. We got over it, though. There was never a full rupture. I knew my parents were disappointed in me and mad at me sometimes, but they had the ability to forgive. They loved me enough that it was safe to rebel. They gave enough safety that we could fight, and I never felt I would be kicked out of the family. I didn't want to be kicked out of the family, and they didn't want to kick me out. And now we see more eye to eye."

Fred Barnes's parents were wise enough to let him know it was safe to rebel a bit. They didn't compromise their standards. They let him know they disagreed with him. They even fought with him. But they never let their disagreements with him or their disappointment in him be so consequential that he felt he was no longer loved, no longer part of the family. And the safety he felt in that relationship was strong enough to draw him back into closer relationship once he grew up a little, became less vulnerable to the dictates of his peers, less driven to rebel for rebellion's sake.

In retrospect, Fred Barnes views his youthful rebellion as relatively mild. But sometimes a child's rebellion is so severe, so disruptive, that some version of "tough love" may be the only answer. Persistent drug or alcohol abuse, violence, or criminal behavior can't be supported. Sometimes kicking an adolescent—or grown—child out of the house is a necessary strategy for making him or her face up to the consequences of untenable behavior. But kicking children out of the house is very different from kicking them out of the family. At some level, even the most seemingly untractable, rebellious, hateful children want to know—need to know—that they can be safe. Safe in the love of their parents.

Safe to Fail

Janet Getz grew up in a family of achievers. Her father was an executive with a major oil company. Her mother is an energetic natural leader who started and ran a number of volunteer causes in several different communities and countries. Her two sisters are both physicians. As for her own life, Getz says, "I tend either to do wonderfully or bomb." One of her more memorable bombs was in graduate school, when she failed her master's exams. After she found out, Getz worried that her super-achiever father wouldn't love her anymore. How could he, when he was so intelligent and successful himself? How could he, when he had such high expectations of her? But she finally worked up the nerve to tell him about the exams—and her fears. He was adamant in his unwavering love for her. "How could you possibly think that whether or not you failed these exams would make a difference in my love for you?" he asked incredulously. Reassured of her safety in the face of failure, Getz went on and got a master's degree in another field, education, where she is flourishing.

Reflecting on that situation, Getz realizes that her father's unconditional love, love that she momentarily doubted but never lost, made it safe for her to pick herself up and try again: "That experience caused me to say to myself, 'Does God think any less of me because of my failure? Does my earthly father? Am I valuable?' Because of my strong background from my parents, who communicated so strongly the sense that who you are as a person is valuable, I could go on. It was hard to take another set of master's exams, but when I did, I got the highest score. But that doesn't make me a different person. It wouldn't have mattered if I didn't get a master's degree. I got a jolt to my system, but since I was grounded, it was okay. If you have people who love you regardless of what you do, as God does, you can come back from the depression I know hits a lot of people when they fail. I thank my parents for that."

Safe to Change and Grow

It must have been hard for Gretchen Ziegenhals's parents when she suddenly became enamored with the tenets of feminist theology. Hadn't they raised her to respond to God as a loving father? It couldn't have been easy for them to sit and listen as she argued passionately for her newly found views. But they did listen. And they continued to accept her and love her, a young woman who had grown to be very different from the little girl who used to pray to her heavenly Father.

It must have been hard for Brenda Watkin's parents when she went away to college and came back with a veneer of sophistication that sometimes bordered on a sense of superiority. How did her mother feel when she looked at this polished young woman and thought about the little girl who used to snuggle up against her on the couch? What did she feel, she who had so little education, who worked intermittently cleaning the homes of rich families, when Brenda went off to study at Oxford? Pride, no doubt. But perhaps a bit of sadness too at the gulf of experience that inevitably separated them. No matter, she never stopped supporting and encouraging her.

How did Janet Getz's parents feel when all three of their daughters grew up to be outspoken evangelicals despite their upbringing in a mainline Protestant denomination? Getz's parents are warm Christians and active church people, but the language and urgency of evangelicalism are somewhat foreign to them. And yet, says Getz, "We've been allowed to become different from them. In so many families, you can never leave or grow up. We've been allowed to grow up and be our own people, to have ideas and thoughts and hopes and dreams that are different from those they might have wanted for us. But we're loved and cared for and valued."

To feel loved and cared for and valued is to feel safe. Even good parents can't always assure their children's physical safety. They can't always maintain daily routines or carry on beloved traditions. When a grandparent dies or an uncle moves away or a favorite Christmas ornament breaks, traditions can be broken too. Parents can't always keep their promises. As much as they try to be dependable, traffic jams can make them late, circumstances can intervene. But ultimately, children feel safe when they know they are loved, even when they rebel, even when they disagree, even when they fail, even when they grow and change.

Make your children feel safe. Do what you can to assure their physical safety, and create an environment that provides emotional safety. Observe ritual, routine, and tradition. Do your best to be dependable. Let your children talk to you, and listen to them when they do. Give them some freedom to disagree and even rebel a little bit without fear of being kicked out of the family. Allow them to change and grow and fail. Above all, let them know that, no matter what they do, you love them.

• NINE •

Model a Good Marriage

My parents loved each other, that was quite obvious. Dad would always come up and pat Mom on the back and give her a big hug and kiss. He'd tell me why he loved her in front of her. And Mom would always say, "Oh, Dan."

Judy Anderson

My parents were married fifty years. As late as their fiftieth year, they'd sit down on the couch, and my dad would put his arm around my mom. It wasn't a mushy kind of thing, but you just knew they felt affection for each other. My dad would chuck her under the chin sometimes. After forty-five years, he was still doing that. I never heard either of them tell the other one, "Yes, I love you," but there was no question in my mind. It was like Fiddler on the Roof. *"Do you love me?" "Why are you asking me? We've been married fifty years!" That kind of affection.*

Lowell Olberg

My parents were head over heels in love with each other. They're still that way. They've been married forty years, and my dad still thinks he got lucky. He said that out loud and repeatedly demonstrated it.

O'Ann Steere

IT'S A FUNNY THING about children: they seem to want their parents to love each other almost as much as they want their parents to love them. Psychologists say it relates to a child's need for a sense of safety and security. Kids want to know not only that their parents will protect them, listen to them, accept them, and love them but also that they'll *stay together*. Children are keen observers of gestures of affection between their parents, of signs of commitment, of the way they disagree, of how they communicate. Children notice whether or not their parents hold grudges. They are appalled, but secretly pleased, at evidence of sexual chemistry between their parents. They watch how their parents get things done. They learn important lessons, negative and positive, by observing the way their parents work together and support, or don't support, each other.

Children who know their parents love each other not only feel secure but also develop a sense of hope about the future. As Kathy Beito says, "Because of my parents' marriage, I know marriage is good. I think that's about as positive as you can get, to be able to see how wonderful it is to be with someone for thirty-five years and to see how that strengthens as the years go on." No wonder so many grown children said that their parents' marriage was a crucial part of their parenting.

DEMONSTRATING LOVE

Over and over, grown children of good parents told me about how important it was for them to see the love between their parents. It made them feel good, secure, safe. But they never would have observed that love if their parents hadn't *demonstrated* it. It's not enough for a husband and wife to love each other. They have to show it—in front of their kids. Couples show love in many different ways: with words, physical affection, thoughtful gestures. Most children sense these various languages of love.

Loving Words

Much has been written about the positive effect of loving words in marriage. What is less recognized is the positive effect on children of hearing loving words expressed between their parents. But children of good parents told me repeatedly how important it was to hear their parents speak of their love for each other, as Timothy Johnson's parents did, for example. "My parents clearly cared about each other and were attentive to each other," says Johnson. "My father in particular would verbalize how much he appreciated my mother. He expressed it more than she did verbally, although she made it clear in other ways. My father would often say, almost in these exact words, 'I married the best woman in the world.' I think that contributes to an overall sense of security that's so important to a child."

Physical Affection

Openly displayed physical affection between parents also contributes to a child's sense of security. Grace Ketterman reflects, "One of my favorite memories is from the Sunday-morning scene. The whole family would be getting ready for church, and I would be ready for Sunday school, sitting in a little rocking chair. I would see my father and mother emerge from their bedroom in the little alcove—I'm sure they didn't know I was there—and my father would put his arms around Mother and look at her so tenderly and would give her a little kiss. I felt so safe and secure."

Dick Chase says his parents' open expressions of affection had a positive effect on him, even though they sometimes made him a bit impatient. "I remember almost every morning

Dad would kiss Mom before he went out to the barn, and he would greet her with a kiss when he came back at night," recalls Chase. "I don't remember them being overly affectionate, but when we were about to leave the house to do something like put the horses in the truck or go out to the high pasture to bring some cows in, I remember thinking, *What are they doing in there?* I'd come around to find them hugging and kissing or something. I couldn't understand that. I was ready to go."

When parents express their love for each other through words *and* physical affection, the message they send their children is doubly powerful. Jay Kesler comments, "I never remember a meal when my father didn't get up from the table, kiss my mother, thank her for the meal, and tell her he loved her in front of us children. His love for her and hers for him was something we children saw often. They were unashamed to show affection in front of us. We assumed all parents loved each other this way."

Loving Actions

For many people, and many families, actions truly speak louder than words. Children who observe their parents behaving thoughtfully and lovingly toward each other are remarkably attuned to the love behind the gestures. "My parents' marriage wasn't perfect," Grace Ketterman observes, "but especially when I was little and most moldable, it was wonderful. My father was very protective of my mother. He took care of her. One year she was quite ill with a chronic heart problem. He took over the household tasks and even baked pies and bread. It was one of many ways he evidenced love and care for her."

FIGHTING RIGHT

A friend of mine has only one mild criticism of the parents he clearly loves and respects: they rarely fought in front of the children. Some people might consider that a great strength. But my friend wonders if it contributed to what he believes is his excessively acute aversion to confrontation. "I didn't have much modeling of how to handle conflict," he observes, "so I grew up with the notion that conflict is a bad thing. It's still hard for me to deal with today."

While it is clearly destructive for children to witness emotional or physical violence between their parents, it can be a very good thing for kids to see their parents disagree and then work through their disagreements. Children who see their parents fight fairly—and then make up—learn that conflict isn't necessarily dangerous, that even people who love each other need to confront each other sometimes. And I suspect that watching people you love, and who love each other, become reconciled after a temporary emotional distancing is an important picture of how we can be reconciled to a God who loves us. I wonder if we can ever really believe at a deep emotional level in the possibility of a restored relationship with God if we've never witnessed emotional separation, reconciliation, and restoration in our own families.

In any case, many grown children of good parents indicated how much they appreciated that their parents taught them by example that disagreements aren't necessarily bad, that conflict is not antithetical to love, and that conflict doesn't need to be destructive. Janet Getz, for example, says that while her parents didn't agree all the time, they were able to work out their occasional differences in constructive ways. "We saw our parents working things through," she says, "but they weren't vicious. They didn't charge each other with 'You always' or 'I hate this.' They didn't use words that would scare a child. We could see them saying, 'This is what I hear you saying . . .' They were good examples of how you can be different and confront one another and still resolve things. I was never afraid that they wouldn't resolve things. I never had to worry about something like divorce."

It probably never occurred to Donald Cole's parents to say, "This is what I hear you saying . . ." during a disagreement. Sometimes they just plain got angry at each other. But they and their children lived securely in the knowledge that an occasional blowup wasn't a threat to their marriage commitment. "I remember once we were driving on a dirt highway in Canada," recalls Cole. "There were no paved highways in that part of Ontario, and Dad was driving too fast. Mother complained, and they got in a fight. We got to some town, and she said, 'Let me out.' So he let her out, drove around the block, and picked her up."

There may be a fine line between healthy modeling of constructive conflict and unhealthy bickering and fighting. Taking a class in or reading a book about interpersonal communication skills may help to define the difference. But even parents who sometimes lapse into a negative form of conflict don't necessarily traumatize their children. In fact, if the parents continue loving and forgiving one another, their conflicts can sometimes teach their children important lessons.

"My parents were a little fussy at times," recalls Brenda Watkins, "but if anything good came out of that, it was the knowledge that you can bicker without it having to be physical or destructive. You can disagree and have emotion about that, but the world doesn't have to fall apart. Disagreement doesn't have to be abusive."

Setting an Example of Forgiveness

Madeleine L'Engle's parents were more than a little fussy, but their world didn't fall apart over an argument either. Their marriage was extremely volatile, says L'Engle, mainly because her father was an extraordinarily volatile man. "But," she says, "he was a wonderful example in many ways because he blew his top and then the sun came up and it was over. My parents never held on to recriminations. They didn't dig at each other day after day. There was a blowup, and it was finished."

Children aren't as upset by their parents' arguments as they are by what they perceive as the potential consequences of those arguments. <u>When parents make it clear that their conflicts have no impact on their ultimate commitment to each other, kids stop worrying</u>. Nancy Swider-Peltz, for example, says that even though her parents fought with each other from time to time, she never felt any sense of instability. "Because of their overall love and commitment, I never feared that their arguments would ever lead to anything," she explains.

More About Forgiveness

It's one thing to forgive your spouse after a blowup about whose turn it is to drop the kids off at school. It's another thing to muster the will to forgive after a major failure or breach of trust. And even good parents do fail sometimes. Sometimes they fail miserably, even sinfully. But parents who can forgive each other and go on not only model God's forgiveness, they make a lifelong impression on their children.

Louis McBurney's father's failure was much more hurtful than just blowing up at his wife. He had an affair with another woman. But his repentance and his wife's forgiveness had a lasting impact on McBurney and his siblings. "My mother told him he had to make a choice," says McBurney. "It was either her and the boys, or the other woman. He couldn't have both. He decided in the right direction, but my parents went through some tough times and made the marriage work." Eventually, says McBurney, his parents established a remarkably loving relationship.

McBurney's mother undoubtedly suffered great heartache over her husband's infidelity. She would have been justified in ending their marriage. But she chose to forgive her husband, to give him another chance—and to give her children the gift of an intact, two-parent family.

STAYING COMMITTED

Fortunately, infidelity is still the exception more than the rule in marriage. But few married couples skate through life without hardship or pain. And the irony about difficulty, of course, is that it can strengthen a marriage or destroy it. Couples who face hardship with the determination to stick together and to stay committed teach their children an important lesson in perseverance and give them the security of knowing they won't be abandoned. That's why Nancy Swider-Peltz was never terribly troubled by her parents' occasional arguments. She knew they would never give up or split up. "We knew they would never leave us," she says. "We knew they were committed, and they taught that commitment meant no options."

Good parents know that staying committed to each other is one of the most wonderful gifts they can give their children. Kathy Beito says her parents made a huge impression on her by their mutual support through difficult times, like when her mother went back to school after years of being at home. "She went back to get a master's degree, which meant she had to be gone a lot," Beito recalls. "I think she was the first woman in our area to do that. It was hard on my dad, but he really did support her. Later, when my dad was diagnosed with Parkinson's disease, I saw how Mom reacted: she was with him for the long haul."

The repercussions of any couple's marriage commitment are often felt for more than one generation. Harold Best, for example, says he attributes the stability of his own marriage in large part to the modeling he got from his parents. "The maturity of my parents' commitment to each other, their *absolute* commitment, is a behavior that was imprinted on me before it ever became doctrinally or existentially mine to prove out in my own marriage," he observes. "I was brought up to know that, whether or not my love wobbles, there are no options. I was brought up to enjoy the fact that my mother and father never contemplated the options because they were bound together ethically and therefore in a loving-kindness at which they had to work—as my wife and I do. My wife and I had a crazy courtship. We got engaged over the phone. I jumped on a train from New York, went back to California, married her, and three days later she was enrolled as a student in New York. I was a freshman faculty member, and she was a brand new wife and student in a strange place. I remember wondering at one point if I'd made a bad choice. Could we be happy together? But the imprinting came out. *There's no option. This will work. Work at it.* That has to have come from my parents."

Single Parenting: Another Kind of Commitment

While many grown children of good parents cited their parents' strong marital commitment as one of most wonderful gifts their parents gave them, it is only one of many possible gifts. Life isn't perfect. Parents make mistakes. Marriages break up. And children, most of whom desperately want their parents to be together, usually suffer. But even inherently tragic situations can be redeemed. Single and divorced parents are not automatically disqualified from the possibility of being good parents. Ben Carson's mother is compelling evidence of that.

When Carson was still a young boy, his parents divorced after his mother discovered his father secretly had another wife and family. His mother was then left to raise Carson and his brother alone. Single parenting isn't easy under any circumstances, but it is especially difficult when the circumstances include extreme poverty. Minimally educated, scarcely able to read, Carson's mother worked as a maid to support her boys. She sometimes worked as many as three jobs to keep food on the table. But tired as she was from working, she still invested enormous amounts of energy into parenting her children.

She never gave up. She never allowed herself to lapse into a victim mentality. She never accepted her less-than-ideal family circumstances as an excuse for letting down on her job as a parent, even though it would have been completely understandable if she had. She knew she couldn't be a father to her boys, but she was determined to be the best mother she could possibly be. And today, her sons honor her, love her, and bless her name.

FUNCTIONING AS A TEAM

The Genesis story of Adam and Eve has implications beyond the explanation it offers for how we humans came to be so flawed and broken. It also gives us a picture of the partnership God intended between man and woman. Before Adam and Eve succumbed to temptation, they were a wonderful team. Given a joint mandate to subdue the earth, they worked together to fulfill it. Made of the same stuff—Eve was after all fashioned from Adam's bone and flesh—they were companions who eased what would otherwise have been each other's unbearable loneliness.

We, of course, live after the Fall. Ours is a broken world. But we can still work toward God's ideal. And part of that ideal is that husbands and wives should be a team. When parents function that way, their children are among the prime beneficiaries. Listen to Jay Kesler reminisce about his parents: "One of the things I appreciated about my parents was their partnership. They were married young: my mother was only fifteen, and my dad was eighteen. They struggled with the economic realities of the Depression together. They moved to northern Wisconsin, having as their only possessions my father's automobile and what few household goods they had. They went to homestead. Eighty acres of land was available to people who would improve it.

"My dad had some experience in farming, but he was unprepared for the northern Wisconsin winter. Nonetheless, the two of them struggled greatly. They traded the car for a team of mules and were stuck with no way to get out except to make their little dream work. They lived in a tent for the first summer, and then my dad built a house out of logs off the land itself. My sister was born the first year, and I was born two years later. From my earliest childhood I thought of my parents as a pioneer couple.

"Even though they sold that farm and moved back to Indiana when I was a small boy, this partnership, this oneness, is probably one of their greatest characteristics as parents. They seemed to talk over everything, to do the smallest things together. I don't think they would have bought an item costing more than a dollar without discussing it. They felt totally accountable to one another."

MODELING HEALTHY SEXUALITY

One of the delightful aspects of God's ideal of oneness in marriage is its physical manifestation: sex. God intended us to enjoy a sexual relationship with our spouse. One of the tragedies of modern Western culture is the false picture it presents of both sex and marriage. With a few exceptions, the primetime television view of sex, for example, seems to be that it is ultimately fun and exciting, but only outside marriage. Only rarely is any sexual chemistry portrayed between husbands and wives. So where can a child get a healthy view of sexuality? If they have good parents, they get it at home.

Jay Kesler recalls that the sense of intimacy between his

parents was very apparent to their children and, later, even to their grandchildren. "My parents modeled sexuality," he says. "When Jane and I had children, we would go on a vacation together with my parents in the Northwoods. We rented a cottage with open loft rooms, and we could hear conversation in other rooms. The kids would listen to my dad kiss my mother goodnight and say a couple of endearing words. They would listen to those words and whisper to us that they heard Grandpa kiss Grandma. Even to this day they look on that as one of the most wonderful things, that their grandma and grandpa loved each other and kissed each other in bed, and they could hear them talking. As for myself, I always felt that intimacy was very real between my parents."

O'Ann Steere's parents weren't very good at sitting down and giving "health lectures," she says, but like Jay Kesler's parents, they modeled a healthy sexuality. "From an early age I knew there was something going on with them," says Steere, "that there was a chemistry there. They weren't overtly, obnoxiously sexual, but we knew something was going on. I was in high school before I figured out why Mom and Dad took a nap every Sunday afternoon. I used to think these grownups were so weird," she laughs. "'These people take a nap every Sunday! They go in their room and lock the door and take a nap!' And there's still chemistry between them."

Wise parents strike an appropriate balance between modesty and openness about sex. Kesler comments, "My parents never ran around in front of us unclothed or partially clothed, but if we asked questions, we got straight and matter-of-fact answers." A little lightheartedness from time to time doesn't hurt, either.

Good parents present sex not as a mysterious and forbidden subject but as a natural, God-given gift. "My parents didn't make sex a taboo thing," says nurse and mother Janice Rohne Long. "My sister and I always looked forward to getting our period, for example, because my parents talked about it as the time when we became a young lady. My dad would tease and say things like, 'We should have had stock in a Kotex company.' They made things like that just a natural part of life."

SUPPORTING EACH OTHER

Good parents don't always agree, but they do support each other as much as possible. The root of that support seems to be a deep respect for the other person, a respect that gets communicated to their kids.

Mary O'Connor says her parents' mutual respect was one of the most noticeable characteristics of their marriage. She was impressed, for example, at the way her mother reacted when her father made a significant job change, a change that held potential for much stress. O'Connor recalls, "My mom took us all aside, and without making a big deal of it, said, 'Your dad is changing jobs, and it's going to be different in many ways. It could be hard on him because he's got some adjustments to make. I want you kids to be understanding and supportive.' That made such an impression on me. I thought, *It's going to be hard on her too, but she's really supportive of him.* And he always was of her too. He is a big fan of hers. He thinks she is the smartest woman in the world, and he can't stop telling how great she is."

Gretchen Ziegenhals has similar memories of her parents. "My parents respected each other as well as loved each other," she says. "I think that was really important for me to see. My father was very proud of all my mother did with her choir and was very supportive of her physically—singing in the choir, being there with us, and not caring if we had hamburgers and applesauce ten nights in a row when she was doing something else. And I know my mom simply adored my father. It was very obvious to us. She respected him and thought he was the end of the world."

One of the most obvious ways in which parents can support each other is by respecting each other's decisions, especially when they relate to their children. For example, wise parents, like O'Ann Steere's, don't let their children get away with the divide-and-conquer strategy of manipulating parental decision making. "An unpardonable sin in my childhood was trying to split the parents," explains Steere. "If we got caught having asked one parent for an answer already and trying to play the end against the middle, we were dead."

Likewise, good parents support each other's style of discipline. "My parents were very together," observes Jay Kesler. "Neither one allowed us to get by with something the other would not have let us do. They supported each other. We couldn't conceive of them disagreeing about discipline. There was no sense in arguing. They were unified."

CLARIFYING ROLES

One other characteristic of parents who manage to forge a strong marriage is one that isn't necessarily thought of much in an era when both husbands and wives have careers: role definition. Especially once they become parents, husbands and wives have to get things done. And in order to get things done, it's necessary to figure out who's responsible for what. It doesn't seem to matter much how the roles are assigned— although it matters to individual couples—but clarity of roles is an important component of a strong marriage.

Jay Kesler observes, "My parents had clear ideas about male and female roles. Dad worked, did all the physical things, all the painting, screens, windows, roof repairs, hole digging. Mother did all the domestic tasks. These seemed to be their domains, though on occasion, Dad would do something for her. For instance, he'd say, 'Elsie, why don't you sit down and read the paper, and I'll do the dishes.' Or he might come home from work and find the lawn mowed. I decided this was an excellent role model. It gave an opportunity to say 'I love you' by doing these things for each other, in contrast to today's model, which seems to be so filled with resentment. People seem so angry and resentful because of blurred roles, because they haven't defined their roles. I don't think there's anything right or wrong about particular roles, but it's wrong not to understand what your division of labor is."

As Kesler points out, there's nothing magic about any one model for dividing up roles and tasks, but finding a division of labor both spouses agree on *is* important. It eliminates unnecessary battles and teaches kids an important lesson in how to cooperate to get things done.

PRIORITIZING THEIR OWN RELATIONSHIP

Probably one of the biggest mistakes well-intentioned couples make when they become parents is trying so hard to be good moms and dads that they forget to work at keeping their marriage strong. But child-centered families aren't necessarily the healthiest families. As O'Ann Steere says of herself and her siblings, "It gave us a very secure feeling that our mom and dad, not us children, were the center of our home." Although kids need lots of love and attention, they can feel unduly pressured if one or both of their parents are looking to them—instead of a spouse—for their primary companionship, support, and intimacy. Kids also need to know that they've got something to look forward to. And one of the best things to look forward to is a happy, loving marriage.

Forging a strong marriage and keeping it strong requires effort. O'Ann Steere's parents' close relationship didn't just happen. Rather, her parents made it happen. They made sure they had time alone together on a regular basis. They went out on dates. They took mini-vacations by themselves.

Steere's father, who owned a small business, took every Tuesday afternoon off just to be with Steere's mother.

Keri Menconi's parents helped each other out with household tasks. They "looked out for each other." They talked to each other, not the national average of sixteen minutes a day but, according to Menconi, sometimes "hours on end."

Brenda Weaver's father traveled a lot, but every night he was gone, he would call his wife. "They talked together nearly every day," says Weaver. "They spent a lot of couple time together. They went out to dinner or went away for a weekend. They held hands. They went out of their way to do things for each other. I've often shed tears because I'm afraid I won't be in a relationship as good as I've seen, and I've seen what I consider to be incredible."

It's as important to your children that you love your spouse as it is that you love them. So if you want to be a good parent, work at your marriage. Demonstrate your love for each other in a visible way. Fight right—and then forgive. Let your kids know you're committed. Work as a team. Model healthy sexuality. Support each other. Clarify your roles. Prioritize your marriage relationship.

Grown children of good parents say it's important.

TEN

Take Time to Spend Time with Your Children

My dad and I were playing tennis in the park, and the football coach stopped by and made a comment about how neat it was that father and son were playing tennis together. I thought, Yeah, that is neat. My dad's a good dad. He really takes time.

Jon Ebersole

WHEN HIS CHILDREN reached a certain age, Steve Roskam's dad, a successful salesperson, realized that his career was threatening his relationship to his kids. In order to advance much further, he was going to have to spend a lot more time traveling. So he went to his boss and told him, "Don't promote me anymore. Just base my compensation on what I earn in sales." Steve Roskam has never forgotten that his dad sacrificed career advancement for something he believed was much more important: spending time with his kids.

I'm not sure I ever really believed in the notion that when it comes to spending time with kids, quality is more important than quantity. If I ever did, I don't now. That's because so

158

many children of good parents have told me <u>one of the things</u> <u>they appreciated most about their parents was the amount of</u> <u>time they spent with them</u>.

<u>It seems to be terribly important to spend big chunks of</u> <u>time with your kids</u>—talking with them, working with them, <u>playing with them</u>. Especially playing with them.

I was in the middle of interviewing Donald Cole when his effervescent wife, Naomi, burst into the room and the conversation. She had overheard us talking about the characteristics of good parents and couldn't restrain herself any longer.

"If there's one thing I wish I'd known earlier about parenting, it's the importance of being fun to live with," she emphasized. "<u>Early in our family life, I was so worried about</u> <u>our kids going astray that I didn't focus nearly enough on fun.</u> <u>But through the years, I've realized how important it is to be</u> <u>fun to live with</u>."

Grown children of good parents confirm Cole's view, so much so that I've come to this conclusion: if you want to create for your children positive memories that will last a lifetime, figure out ways to have fun with them.

SPEND TIME HAVING FUN

"We had a fun family," says Nancy Tecson. "Mom made sure we had tennis lessons, and even though I was shy about it, my sister and I have enjoyed tennis for years. Mom insisted we have swimming lessons. Later on, when I was in junior high, we ended up building a pool. Mom and Dad both loved the water and water sports. My dad likes boats a lot and just being in the water, so we did water skiing. We played games. We spent a lot of time in recreation, which has been a great thing, especially in our teen years. Family vacations were a time we did a lot of recreation. We would even cook together and clean up together; we would make a game out of things.

We just had a feeling of fun in our family. Even if it was a mundane kind of chore, we ended up joking around and laughing."

Doug Anderson is the first to admit his parents weren't perfect. He still smiles, for example, about the time he jumped into the lake near their vacation home to save his eighteen-month-old brother from drowning—and was rewarded with a scolding from his mother for getting his clothes wet! But Anderson has wonderful memories of his childhood and is quick to voice appreciation for his parents. He has a particularly strong bond with his father, a successful electronic engineer, who to an unusual degree arranged his life so he could engage in recreational activities with his son.

"Probably the first thing I think of when I think of my dad is his willingness to introduce me to different recreational activities when I was a child," says Anderson. "Recreation was my dad's big strength. I've tried nearly every sport—skiing, scuba diving, canoeing, cross-country skiing, racquetball, handball, tennis, mountain climbing—just everything. My dad introduced me to all of them. My dad was very handy, and he picked up an old junky aluminum boat and made it into a water-ski boat. So at the age of five or six, I learned how to water ski. My dad pulled me over a water-ski jump at the age of nine.

"We had a cottage on a lake in Indiana, and in the summers, my dad would work Tuesdays, Wednesdays, and Thursdays and take Mondays and Fridays off so he could have a four-day weekend," Anderson continues. "He did that the whole summer, and he spent much of the time taking me here and there, doing things. We really had a close bond based on activities we did together, activities that were always really exciting and fun."

Anderson's reflections on the recreational life he shared with his father are remarkably similar to reflections of other children of good parents. Kathy Beito remembers skiing and snowmobiling with her parents in the winter and boating and fishing in the summer. Betty Fountain remembers hours and hours with her dad, playing games and listening to him read books aloud. Mary O'Connor remembers that every Sunday her father would take her and her siblings to the park to play, and when she hit her teen years, he helped her build a sailboat. Keri Menconi remembers constant outings and family trips to go hiking, swimming, and canoeing.

Why do these memories stand out so sharply in the minds of these grown children of good parents? I think Kathy Beito expresses it well, "Having fun together gave us a bond that just doesn't happen if it's all work and no play," she says.

Fun Doesn't Have to Be Expensive

While many grown children speak appreciatively of the time they spent with their parents in activities like skiing and boating, parents of any income level can have fun with their kids. As Jay Kesler points out, a modest income doesn't have to be a deterrent to shared recreation. "We were a lower-class, blue-collar family," he observes about his own upbringing, "but we did lots of fun things that weren't terribly expensive. My mother made baloney sandwiches, and we would have picnics in the park. We camped out at a lake and fished together. I spent a lot of time with my dad. When I was a little boy, I used to sit in the bottom of the boat while he fished, and I'd go to sleep. We even cooked in the boat. We would have a gas stove in the middle seat, and we'd fry eggs on it and have a little picnic right there in the boat. My parents were fun."

While a big income isn't necessary for family fun, a relaxed attitude is—or at least it helps. Louis McBurney recalls, for example, that his mother wasn't overly worried about the kids creating a mess in the house, and she wasn't terribly concerned about maintaining her dignity. "My mother let us have freedom about play," he explains. "How the house looked wasn't so important that we couldn't play. And in the early years, she would get down on the floor and play with us. I can remember building tents out of blankets and tables, and she'd be down there crawling around with us. We would run string from one chair leg to another across the room. We played games—dominoes, forty-two, Old Maid, Hide and Seek, and Kick the Can. And she'd play with us."

CREATE AN ATMOSPHERE THAT ATTRACTS KIDS

Wise parents make their home the fun place to be. People repeatedly remarked, as if it had just occurred to them, that somehow their house was the place their friends always ended up. "My house was the place to go on a Friday or Saturday night," says Jody Hedberg, who grew up in a small Indiana town. "I didn't have to plan a special party. After the ball games, we would all just go home, and Mom would make chili or fry hamburgers. The guys would push the furniture back against the wall and literally roll up the rugs, and we danced. It didn't bother my mother at all. Most of the kids' parents were friends of my parents, and the adults would all meet in the kitchen. My mother would fry oysters, and they'd be sitting on the tabletops or countertops while the kids would be in the living room, dining room, and den.

"I wonder why my friends always came to my house instead of other houses," Hedberg muses. "It happened so much I sometimes thought, *Hey, I'd like to go to somebody else's house once in a while*. I think maybe it was because neither my father or my mother was condemning or complaining. My mom sure had the messes to clean up, but she never complained. I think she was glad we were home."

"Our home was the drawing place for our peers," remembers Grace Ketterman. "We had incredible parties. Huge scavenger hunts out in the country, sledding parties in the winter, with hot chocolate and popcorn afterward. I was very fortunate. Many of my friends' parents were very strict. They weren't allowed to go out and play on Sundays. But in our family, we were allowed to play on Sunday and whoop it up."

THE SECRET TO GETTING THROUGH ADOLESCENCE

Having fun may be the secret to maintaining a good relationship with your kids during the adolescent years. Some friends once told me that after observing many different families—including families headed by what they considered to be model parents in almost every way—they'd come to the conclusion that the ones who got through adolescence with the fewest scars were those in which the parents and the teenagers were able to participate in recreation together. Those who didn't have much fun together—even those families headed by parents who seemingly did everything else right—went through some stormy years. My conversations with adult children who say they have good parents confirm this observation. Apparently, shared fun can provide a common ground during a time when none might exist otherwise.

Take David Heim's family, for example. Despite his bent for independent thinking, Heim says he never felt the need to rebel against his father, a Baptist minister, or his mother, a home-economics teacher. It was just too much fun being with them. "I just really enjoyed being with my family," says Heim. "We did many recreational activities together, and even in high school I enjoyed family outings. We used to go to the Y every Friday night as a family. And especially during the warm weather months, we went to our summer house in Lake Champlain. Summer vacations were almost always spent as a family doing stuff like fishing, canoeing, or hiking."

MAKING FUN

Parents can't spend all their time playing, but good parents do seem to go to considerable effort to create fun for their kids. Joan Beck remembers that while her father didn't have much time to play with his children because of the demands of his job, he made sure they had plenty of opportunities to create their own fun. "One time he got some lumber," Beck recalls, "and made us four bushel baskets full of these wonderful blocks. We would build great castles with moats and mazes that we were allowed to keep standing in the house as long as we wanted. He also built us a raised sandbox with white sand and built a swing and embedded it so strongly in the back yard that it's still there."

Mary O'Connor's father decided his kids should have a swimming pool, a luxury he couldn't afford. "So he took out a shovel and made a swimming pool," O'Connor says, still amazed many years later. "It took two summers, but we had a pool. In fact, we had a whole park of things: a merry-go-round, a seventeen-foot sliding board. And whenever it snowed, my dad would put a big sled on the back of his jeep, and all the neighborhood kids would come, and we'd go flying around the woods on the back of the sled for hours and hours."

Gregg Roeber's father didn't build a swimming pool, but he crafted some toys that pleased his son as much as any pool could have. "One Christmas he made me a set of different-sized wooden swords," Roeber explains. "One was shaped like a Roman legionnaire's sword. Another was a huge saber. Those were extraordinary things, and I was delighted with them."

Good parents can add to the joy of their children's recreation by enjoying it along with them. Kids thrive when they know their parents delight in delighting them. Luis Palau, for example, says that part of the joy he derives in thinking back on family fun times comes from the memory of his parents' joy in providing them. "We did a lot of plays and skits in our family," he recalls. "We would play musical chairs, and my parents would involve themselves in that. Sometimes my dad would play soccer with us on weekends. Occasionally my parents were part of our fun, but mostly they just looked on and applauded. They just glowed at the kids' laughter."

BE ACCESSIBLE FOR FUN

Good parents don't just schedule recreation times that tend to be geared to their own agendas. They make sure they're accessible to play on their kids' timetable, as Jon Ebersole's father did.

"My dad was a doctor and had a busy schedule," recalls Ebersole, "but I don't remember him ever saying he didn't have time to play. I can remember going to him—he'd be sitting in the family room reading a newspaper or magazine—and I'd ask him to play with me. He wouldn't say, 'Just a minute.' He would put down the magazine, and we'd go out, which is what I needed as a young kid of five or six years old. We would play catch, baseball, or tennis together. I don't remember this, but I'm told he'd come home when we were real little, and after being gone all day, he'd get down on the floor and play with us. Mom said he was very tired, but it gave her a break."

RESPOND TO KIDS' INTERESTS

Good parents are responsive to their kids' interests, even when they don't share those interests. Ron Hutchcraft's mother probably had more fascinating ways to spend her time than playing cowboy or "street-fixing man" with her son. But Hutchcraft says she always had time to engage in his fantasy role playing. And Janet Getz is still amazed that her dignified, executive father let down his hair enough to practice disco dancing with her when she took a course in high school. "I would come home from class, and my dad, who at the time was in his early fifties and weighed about 240 pounds, would say, 'Show me those dance steps,'" she says. "He would become my partner. This huge bear of a man would be bouncing around as I played disco records!"

RESPOND TO YOUR KIDS' CHANGING INTERESTS

Smart parents respond to their children's changing ideas of fun. They know that just because their children enjoyed going to the playground last year doesn't mean they want to do that this year. They grow along with their children. O'Ann Steere recounts, "I give my parents a lot of credit for being aware when our ideas of recreation changed. They were in their forties when they took up downhill skiing. My dad said, 'This is what my kids want to do, so I'm going to learn how to do it.' So we had our family reunions out in Colorado. As kids, we loved to go tenting, but when that wasn't very exciting to us anymore, they were willing to change. Instead of wringing their hands, they found out what we wanted to do. We played pool together in the basement. We went snowmobiling. On a winter weekend we went to a motel with a swimming pool. Instead of insisting we have family fun in the summer and do all the things we had always done, they were willing to do something different."

WORK TOGETHER

Good parents also spend time working with their children. Luis Palau's father would take his son with him when he went out to milk the cows or supervise field work. "I'd sit on the tractor and feel like a big man," Palau recalls. Mary O'Connor helped her father plant a hundred trees in their huge back yard. And every night during the summer, they would carry out buckets to water them. Elaine Kirk worked in the fields with her farmer father and helped him build fences. By the time she was eight years old, she was already driving the truck. "We'd be digging holes for the fences, and I'd move the truck to the right spot," she explains.

Even though life on a farm may seem more conducive to working with your children than other styles of living, some parents manage to arrange their lives so they can at least work near their children. Brenda Watkins' father took her along on his pastoral calls and even included her in his meetings. "I have these memories of my dad including me in his whole life," says Watkins. "I'd go with him to visit the sick in the hospital. I'd go with him to the funeral home. I'd sit in meetings with him. I remember going to conventions with him to Miami, Omaha, and other places around the country. Whatever he did, I would do."

For Brenda Watkins and other children of good parents, being able to observe their parents doing their work was tremendously valuable. It gave them a unique viewpoint not only of their parents, they say, but also of the world.

TAKE TIME TO TALK AND LISTEN

Joan Beck remembers the dinner hour at her childhood home as a time to argue with her parents, especially her father. And she loved it. She and her sister used to sit at the table long after they had finished eating, debating with their parents about politics, about things happening at school, about events going on in town and in the world. "My sister and I used to say, 'Anything we say will be used against us,'" recalls Beck. "But it happened in an interesting, challenging, learning way. It wasn't anything threatening. I don't remember the subjects we argued about as much as I remember the pleasure of talking at the dinner table. That went on through high school, to the point that I assumed this is what one did before getting up from the table. For us, it was a learning experience. We learned a lot from listening to our parents. I don't know why they listened to us."

Like the Becks, good parents spend time talking with, and listening to, their children. They make their kids feel that their thoughts and opinions are valuable. Jody Hedberg, for example, remembers that her parents included her in their conversations as if she were another adult. "We would talk about a news item or a radio program we were listening to, for example," she says. "Mom told me, 'You know, I always wanted you to feel good about yourself because when I was growing up, children weren't allowed to talk. Children were to be seen and not heard.' She said, 'I was always insecure, and I didn't want you to have that insecurity. I wanted you to feel confident.'"

While Jody Hedberg's parents included her in their world and conversations, David Heim's mother went out of her way to give her son an opportunity to include her in his. "My mom taught school," Heim observes, "and at a certain age we both got home at the same time and had a cup of coffee together. I thought that was really cool. I thought I was really grown up. We would sit there and drink coffee, and I'd hear about her day and she'd hear about mine. She was always interested. Just the fact that she understood high school was a jungle meant a lot to me."

FIND CREATIVE WAYS TO SPEND TIME WITH YOUR KIDS

Having declared the importance of spending large quantities of time with your kids, I have to backpedal a bit. Admonitions on the importance of spending time with your kids can produce guilt for parents who have to work long hours just to make ends meet. For some people, the choice not to travel or work long hours or accept a new position wouldn't result in just lack of promotion, as it did for Steve Roskam's and Dave Handley's dads. It might mean loss of a desperately needed job. And parents have a fundamental responsibility to provide for their children's food, clothing, and shelter.

Be Psychologically Accessible

As I reflect on the spending-time-with-your-kids versus providing-for-your-kids conundrum, I come to this conclusion: while your physical presence with your children is ideal, your psychological accessibility to them can sometimes be almost as good.

Mary Kay Ash's childhood is a fairly dramatic example of this principle. Even though her mother's seven-day-a-week job as a restaurant manager required her to leave the house early in the morning and often not get back until after her daughter had gone to bed, Ash never resented her mother's absence. And she has shown no signs of having suffered from it. The reason, I suspect, lies in at least two factors: first, Ash understood why her mother had to be away so much; and second, her mother was accessible. Ash would call her throughout the day, asking for instructions on how to do various things at home, and somehow her mother always made time to talk with her.

"I didn't see her very much," recalls Ash, "but I was able to call her any time I needed help. To be able to call her and ask her something and have her be so patient with me—those phone conversations were bright spots in my day."

Be Physically Present Despite the Demands of Work

Mary Kay Ash's mother found a way to be present with her child even though she was physically absent because of her work responsibilities. Some parents find ways to be physically present with their children despite their work responsibilities.

I think of Gretchen Ziegenhals's mother, for example, who had a demanding career as director of an internationally recognized choir. Gretchen says she derived tremendous benefits from the fact that she could observe her mother's career. "My mom had an office both at home and at the organization she worked for," says Ziegenhals, "so she was away from home only one day a week or for an occasional meeting. She essentially worked out of the home, which was a great model for me. She believed it was crucial to be there when her kids got home from school because we had the most news right when we walked in the door from school. She knew that if she didn't hear it then, she wasn't going to hear it. So we grew up with a mother who was not only always home but also fully immersed in an incredibly rewarding career. I felt as if she had the best of both worlds, and so did we."

Making the Most of Limited Time

Benjamin Carson's mother wasn't able to be physically *or* psychologically present with her two young sons during the long hours she worked as a maid. Domestic work by its very nature is done in someone else's home, and she would have been fired if she had spent long periods on the phone. Because she often worked two and three jobs to make ends meet, she would sometimes spend entire days away from her sons. But they understood why their mother had to be gone so much, and they appreciated the fact that she made the most of the time they did have together. "My mother could have spent a lot of time with us if she had been willing to accept welfare checks," observes Carson, "but she didn't think that would have been a good example. So she made a trade-off. She spent time with us whenever she wasn't working. And we didn't just sit around. We'd go places. We would go to the zoo, to free museums, to the country to pick apples and grapes. She was very resourceful."

If work and the responsibility to support your family is robbing you of time with your children, try to come up with a creative solution. Maybe you can do some of your work at home. Maybe you can negotiate a flexible arrangement with your employer. Failing that, try to make yourself more psychologically accessible to your children during the day. Not all employers allow personal phone calls, but even a note in a lunch box can help to make a loving connection. And don't forget to make the most of the time you do have with your children. You can create an important bond by responding to your kids' interest in and need for recreational outlets.

FIND A PLACE TO SPEND TIME

Some parents make sure they spend time with their kids by setting aside a place to be together as a family. Take the summer cottage Gretchen Ziegenhals's parents built, for example: "One very important aspect of family time for me was our cottage in New Hampshire," says Ziegenhals. "When they were first married, my parents bought a piece of land up there for a song, not really realizing what they were stumbling on. And then as we were growing up, we continued to go there every summer. We eventually built a cottage that has become a real anchor in our family life because of the sense of place it has given us. I don't think my brother and I have missed more than a summer going back there with our families."

Dave Handley has these memories of his family's fun place. "We had a cottage about an hour and a half away from our home. It was on an island in the middle of a lake. It was like our family. In a sense we too were an island. That cottage said, 'This is us. We're family.'"

So many interviewees spoke of their warm memories of time spent at a family cottage or cabin, that I began to wonder if it's possible to be a good parent without having a vacation home. If that were true, parents with modest incomes would seem to have reason for despair. But there seemed to be little correlation between income and having a place specifically dedicated to recreation. Two interviewees who spoke most fondly of their vacation cottages, for example, came from clergy families—David Heim and Gretchen Ziegenhals. If their experience is any guide, creating a place for fun takes more effort than money; they built their own cottages. Other families might attend the same family camp or rent the same cottage or cabin every year.

In any case, a place to be together doesn't have to be outside the home. It can be, and often is, inside the home. In Janet Getz's family, the "togetherness place" was the kitchen. "We spent a lot of time around the kitchen table," she recalls. "People would just congregate in our huge kitchen. We would choose to do our homework at the kitchen table instead of our rooms, where we had desks, because other people would be there. And on the weekend, somebody might be making bread or jelly or rolling up apples. Even if there was nobody else in the kitchen, you knew somebody would come through."

FIND A SPECIFIC TIME TO BE TOGETHER

Some families set aside a specific time to be together. Often, for example, good parents set aside mealtimes or one particular mealtime as togetherness time. "Mealtimes were very sacred in our family," says Jon Ebersole. "We ate breakfast together and had devotions together in the morning. Most of us came home for lunch. But dinner was a sacred time. The message conveyed was that we were important, that this was important to do."

Gerald Koenig has similar memories. "It was almost unheard of that we would miss a meal with the family," he recalls. "We ate lunch together and supper together. Even as we got into our teen years and became quite involved in athletics, we would work around our schedules and still eat our meals together. It showed that family was important."

Good parents understand the importance of setting aside a specific time for fun. Like vacations. Many people seem to remember family vacations more vividly and positively than almost any other aspect of their childhood. Ron Hutchcraft's comments are typical. "Some of my warmest memories are of family vacations," he says. "We traveled largely around the midwest—Michigan, Wisconsin. Once we went to Washington D.C. When we went to those places, I would write stories about our experiences. I remember writing a story after we went to Colonial Williamsburg."

David Handley recalls that he and his brother "fought like crazy" holed up in the car on their frequent family vacations out West. But, he says, those are the times he remembers best. "Those were family-building times," he reflects. "I have good memories of water skiing together, snow skiing together, playing a lot of golf together. I remember climbing mountains in the West, riding the trolley in San Francisco, going to Alcatraz and Disneyland. My dad even took us to Europe once as a family."

Molly Cline says her parents never missed an opportunity to turn work into play. They had a special knack for turning business trips into vacations. "My parents were very spirited and spontaneous," she says. "My dad was in agricultural work with a baby-food company, so he had to travel all over. Whenever he could make it a fun trip for the whole family, we would all go. We all had chances to go on individual trips with him too. And we always did fun family outings. We went to state parks for day picnics, swimming, eating outside. I remember when I was in about second grade, we went on a family vacation to Niagara Falls. There were all these various restaurants and hot dog stands, but my father wanted to have a picnic. So we went to a local supermarket, bought bread, fresh tomatoes, a jar of mustard, and sandwich meat and had lunch on an old army blanket right there at Niagara Falls."

DOING DIFFERENT THINGS TOGETHER

Good parents know that being together doesn't necessarily mean doing the same things together. Just doing things near each other can be a wonderful thing. Janet Getz reflects, "We spent a lot of time together in the evenings, working in close proximity to each other. My dad would be in one part of the living room, working on stuff for his job, and Mom would be in the dining room, through this huge doorway, working on projects for her work. I would be doing homework on the couch, and my sister would have her books sprawled on the floor. Even though we were working on our own activities, we knew people were there to interact with us. I remember one night Dad said, 'What are you working on?' I said, 'Aw, poetry. I hate it. I can't do it.' He put down his work and came in to help me. That said to me that I was important to him. He wanted to be part of my life. It told me that I was okay, that these people wanted to be with me."

Come to think of it, that may be why spending time with your kids is so important. When you take time to play with them, work with them, talk with them, and listen to them, it gives them an important message: they're okay. These people—their parents—want to be with them.

ELEVEN

Give Your Children Guidance About Money

The main value my parents gave me about money was that it's not important. Things aren't important.

David Heim

Many people in my generation thought it wasn't good to be rich. I grew up thinking it was good to be rich so you could give away a lot of money. In my family, money was to be used in an open, hospitable way.

O'Ann Steere

My parents taught me that if you want money, you go to work. That was where money came from.

Louis McBurney

ONE OF MY REAL quandaries as a parent is what to teach my kids about money. It's a quandary in part because my kids are growing up in very different financial circumstances from those in which I grew up. My father worked for a Christian organization, and like most full-time Christian workers, he

earned very little money. My husband's parents were missionaries, so he grew up in modest circumstances as well. While
neither of us lacked for adequate food, clothing, or shelter, we
had few extras during childhood.

That's not true of our children. While we're far from
wealthy, I sometimes wonder if my husband and I are guilty
of the overindulgence that so often characterizes modern
parenting. I wonder if we're teaching our kids the right values
about money. I wonder if we're teaching them *any* values
about money.

What should we be teaching our kids about money? How
much of it should we be giving them? What's the best way for
them to learn to handle it?

The fascinating thing about money is the power it has over
so many people's lives, whether or not they have very much of
it. But the fascinating thing about grown children of good
parents is how little power money has over them.

Good parents give their kids values about money. Often,
they also teach them practical skills in using money. But what
seems to be most important is the perspective these parents
give their children on the role of money in life. Grown
children of good parents have a healthy respect for money
because they've learned to connect it to work. But they know
it isn't the most important thing in life. So they're free to be
generous and honest—good stewards. Just like their parents.

MONEY VALUES

Good parents differ in their view of money. Some, like Fred
Barnes's parents, think it is a potential source of danger. "I
grew up with the notion that wealth would probably do more
harm than good, that rich people got messed up as a result of
it," explains Barnes. Others see it as a blessing from God, a
gift that can and should be used for his purposes. Evangelist
Luis Palau, son of a successful Argentinean businessperson

says, "My parents showed me that business success and Christianity can go together. You make money to extend the kingdom of God. To be successful in business is an honorable calling."

Diverse as they are in their views, good parents have this in common: they have positive principles about money, and they pass on those principles to their children. One of the most common values among these parents is the conviction that money is a lesser priority in life. Timothy Johnson, for example, says that one of the most important gifts his father gave him was the constant message, both verbally and through the way he lived, that money was not the most important thing in life. "He used to say to us, 'Don't chase the almighty buck. It'll disappoint you,'" recalls Johnson. "I remember that message. I had a sense he lived that way himself. While he wasn't going to take a vow of poverty, his lifestyle indicated that he really didn't care primarily about money."

Good parents clue their children into the fact that, while it's necessary to find a way to make ends meet, money shouldn't be the dominating factor in their choice of a career. Fred Barnes recounts, "I give my parents full credit for the fact that money wasn't a factor in my choosing a vocation. I never thought about making a lot of money. I took a job for $85 a week at a newspaper in South Carolina. My dad never thought about making a lot of money either. Not that he wasn't interested in having any money—he wanted us to be a family that could do things—but he wasn't expecting to get rich."

Good parents teach their children not only how to delight in the material world created by God without longing for material things but also how to be happy even when they're poor. Harold Best's parents didn't have any money. "But they didn't lust after it, and they didn't gripe about it," Best says. "They were as far from being materialists as you can get. But they had a gift for creating a context in which good things were loved without being longed for. As a result, even though my present salary doesn't compare with what I would be earning in another institution, I can't believe how well off I am. I have a very natural, rich aesthetic sense that did not come from Claremont Graduate School or Union Seminary or textbooks or anywhere else. That is a great, great gift."

Luis Palau's family was wealthy until his father died and they lost the income from his successful business. But even after experiencing the comforts of affluence, poverty didn't diminish their joy in life. "A principle I learned from my mother was to be happy even when you are poor," says Palau. "My mother quoted Matthew 6:33 endless times: 'Seek first the kingdom of God and his righteousness and all these things shall be added unto you.' That was a reality to us. We took it seriously, and the Lord never failed us."

THE VALUE OF VALUES

Growing up with parents who taught that money was a lesser priority in life seems to have helped many grown children make vocational choices based on their gifts and interests rather than on financial considerations alone. Take Brenda Watkins, for example, the daughter of an urban pastor father and a full-time mother. After graduating from college, Watkins met a law-school dean who was a man of deep faith and who knew of her interest in working with the African-American community. He started telling her how she could be of service as an attorney, a very attractive idea to a young, gifted, achievement-oriented black woman whose mother had worked as a maid. And while there's little question that she could have been of service as an attorney, Watkins, who had just gone through something of a spiritual renewal, began a process of prayer and reflection on who she was. And she concluded that, while she could have been an attorney, she probably shouldn't be. It was an appropriate vocation for others, but not for her. She chose instead to go into social work, a notably low-paid profession. She doesn't think she could have made that decision if she hadn't had parents who taught her that money isn't the most important thing in life.

"Because of my parents," says Watkins, "it was never a priority for me to have a career that would pay me so many dollars. If it had been more of a priority, I probably would have leaned more toward being a lawyer instead of a college faculty person and counselor. Because of the importance my dad placed on spiritual things, my personal relationship to God became my priority. Because of the influence of my father, I knew the importance of going with your passion, of being of service, and I intentionally made choices consistent with those values."

Nancy Swider-Peltz says she learned her values about money more from her father's example than from his words. A lifelong teacher and coach, Mr. Swider in his later years began telling Nancy and her brothers that it was very important to find a job that paid well, unlike his chosen career. But his kids weren't fooled.

"He never would have said that if he hadn't gotten sick and had to take a loan to pay his hospital bills," observes Swider-Peltz. "We knew he wouldn't have said that twenty years ago because he loved his job. And we all went into some related field. My brothers were both football coaches, and I coach skating. We all respected what he did so much that we took on his profession. So when he would say, 'Why don't you do something that earns more money?' we'd say, 'Dad, you loved what you did! Isn't that a compliment that we respected you so much we're doing what you did?'"

GENEROSITY

While good parents know and teach their kids that money isn't the most important thing in life, they make positive use of what money they have. Because they're not ruled by money, these parents cheerfully share their resources. Because her parents were so unselfish in providing for her, Joan Beck assumed her parents' resources were greater than they actually were. "I realize now that my parents didn't have that much money," she reflects. "I thought they had more than they really did. They were so generous that I always assumed there was lots more there. I found out late in life that they were simply very generous. I was cleaning out my father's house a few years ago and found his checkbook. At one point he had fifty cents in his checking account. It never occurred to me that he was on the edge because he always provided for me so well."

Nancy Swider-Peltz knew early on that her parents had limited resources. And it still touches her that her father, who made a modest income as a teacher, worked so hard to earn a little extra money to provide for his kids' futures. "My dad would give us all his coaching money," she recalls. "He didn't shower on us money that was easy to get; he gave us money we knew was very hard for him to earn. He didn't buy anything for himself. He gave it to us to save for college."

While good parents are as generous as they can afford to be, their generosity is not blind or without limits. Wise parents know that allowing children to be irresponsible with money isn't in their best interest. Jay Kesler's parents, for example, used allowances to teach their children some lessons about money. "When I ran out of money, I was out of money," recalls Kesler. "My parents didn't make loans. We had to wait until payday. We knew what zero meant."

Dick Chase's parents didn't give their children allowances but were almost always willing to underwrite the cost of an occasional malt or hamburger. Still, their generosity had its limits too. "When I was in high school, Dad would give me money for a date, and I didn't have to report back," Chase observes. "I can remember getting a $20 bill one time, for example, easily the equivalent of $75 or $100 today. But I spent all of it, and when I came back the next week, he said, 'I gave you $20 last week. I think that's enough for this month.' I learned pretty quickly that money had to spread out. I learned to handle it carefully." And that, of course, was the whole idea.

STEWARDSHIP

Good parents model and teach stewardship. They let their kids know, by example and by instruction, that God's people are called to use "their" money and resources for his purposes. Luis Palau, for example, recalls that his parents' attitude was, "Everything belongs to the Lord, so you should only keep as much as you need."

"It seemed to me as a child," says Palau, "that everything we owned literally belonged to the church, the kingdom, evangelism. Even though, by local standards, we were wealthy while my dad was living, there was no gloating, no flaunting, no showing off. There was an attitude of humility."

Jon Ebersole says he has a very vivid mental picture that he associates with his parents' stewardship. "I remember Saturday night Dad would sit down and write a check for what I thought was an enormous amount of money," he says. "Week after week, without fail, he would put that in the offering plate. He never said, 'Gee, we could really use this money.' It was never an issue. It was a priority to give money to the church."

Ebersole also recalls that his parents went out of their way to help him develop habits of stewardship. "I don't remember how old I was," he says, "but I had a 35-cent allowance, and I was encouraged to put a dime of that in a missions bank I had. And then every year in Sunday school, we would take the money in for missions. I thought this was great stuff. A dime every week for a year built up to what I thought was quite a bit of money. Ten cents out of 35. I thought, that's just what you do."

Donald Cole still remembers how his father first introduced the subject of giving back to God and initiated what turned out to be an entire life of stewardship. "My dad was sitting in his green leather chair one day, reading his newspaper," Cole recalls, "and I showed him the money I'd earned from a week's work delivering newspapers. I earned about $4.75 delivering seventy-five papers. He looked down at me and said, 'You've earned $4.75. That's good.' And then he said, 'How much of that are you going to give to God?' I hadn't thought of giving anything. But he said, 'Well, part of it belongs to God.' So I started dropping money in the collection box. That's how it all started."

WHERE MONEY COMES FROM

One of the most crucial values good parents teach their children is the notion that money is connected to work. While good parents generously provide for their kids' needs as best they can, they also let their children know that money doesn't just drop out of the sky.

While Jay Kesler's parents gave their children allowances, for example, they connected them to work. "We were all expected to contribute to the family's well-being," explains Kesler. "We all worked to help the family function, and we all got part of the family reward."

Elaine Kirk says her parents never begrudged the price of a ticket for a school activity or an occasional Coke, in part, because she and her sisters worked so hard on their family farm. And when it came time to go away to college, they understood they had to do their part. "We had to earn our own spending money," she observes. "I learned respect for money really fast that way. I waited on tables to pay for my board. It was a case of realizing, if I'm going to eat, I have to work to pay for it."

David Handley's parents might have been able to afford college tuition for all three of their children, but they felt it was important that their kids take on some of the financial responsibility. "My dad let us know we would have to pay for half of our college education ourselves," explains Handley. "He gave us matching grants. So while all the other kids were out taking driver's education, I was out with a summer job. That was a good value fostered there."

TEACHING KIDS HOW TO USE MONEY

Good parents teach their kids not only how to view money but also how to handle it—by giving them an example to follow and opportunities to practice. Many grown children of good parents cited their parents' frugality, for example, as modeling that has influenced their adult lives. Take Benjamin Carson's mother. "She was very thrifty," observes Carson. "Save, save, save was a constant theme. Anybody can take money and throw it away. My mother always said, 'A fool and his money are soon parted.' She was a woman who worked for minimum wages, and yet she always had a car that worked. And she never bought a used car. She always paid cash for every car she got, even if it meant saving every penny she got her hands on for five or six years. She did it.

"We would go to free museums," he continues. "She would try to develop relationships with people who lived out in the country, and we would sometimes go out and pick food in their gardens. For helping to harvest their crops, we would get some of them. She was extremely handy with a sewing machine and needle and thread. She would go through Goodwill and get clothes and patch them up and make them look pretty good. She'd get things from people she worked for. She was extraordinarily resourceful. No one ever had any idea of how poor we really were because of that. Those are lessons that are not lost on a young observant mind, seeing somebody take nothing and make something out of it."

Judy Anderson says her parents were similarly frugal, and their example continues to shape her life to this day. "I think I can count on one hand the number of times I bought a new outfit and paid full price," she says. "Something goes against me in doing that. We always made over clothes when I was growing up. Mom remade several suits that wealthy women had owned, and I always felt good in them. I guess I don't care if somebody else has worn something before. It's no big deal to me. I just feel I'm being a better steward. I feel as if I'm recycling. I think that's a good thing, and I'm glad I grew up not feeling ashamed of it."

The Pros and Cons of Allowances

Interestingly, good parents seem to be divided on the subject of allowances—one of the most common vehicles for teaching kids how to handle money. A number of interviewees said they had allowances as children, but many didn't. Those who did have allowances said it was good practice for managing money in later life. On the other hand, some of those who didn't said depending on their parents to provide was good practice for depending on the Lord.

Janet Getz recalls, "If I needed something, I could talk to Mom or Dad and say, 'I really need this, and this is why.' They would say, 'Okay, here's the money. I trust you to use it.' As a result of that, and my faith, I trust in God to provide for me because he promises he will. It's kind of an unusual outcome, but a very positive one. I knew if I had a need, my earthly father would take care of it. And my heavenly father promises to provide for me too. My trust in that is really high."

Practicing Money Skills

Whether or not they're given an allowance, kids do need practice managing money. Luis Palau first became a money manager at the age of six, when his parents opened a savings account for him at the local bank. They gave him a savings book and encouraged him to check interest rates and look at the way his money grew.

Mary Kay Ash learned money skills very early in life because she was responsible for doing much of the family shopping. The lessons she learned and the experience she gained have stayed with her—even though she's now a woman of wealth. "During the Depression," she recalls, "nobody had any money. So we were very careful and scrupulous with what little we had. When I went to buy groceries, I would go into the corner grocery store and try to stretch the dollar as far as it would go. That has hung over. Even today when I go into grocery stores, I'll pick up three cans of tomatoes and decide which is the best value even though I could buy the store if I wanted to. I still clip coupons. Double coupons and triple coupons. Right now I have an organized file of those things. I go through and pick out coupons. On Friday, I got back nearly six dollars. It's ridiculous, but part of that is the early training of trying to save every penny we had. And in the early days of my business, I'm sure it was part of our success."

Good parents teach their kids to value money, but not too much. They teach them to be generous yet responsible. They show them that while money comes from work, money is only one of many considerations to be taken into account when choosing what kind of work to pursue. They teach their children both the power and the limits of money. They teach them how to view money and how to use it wisely.

In one sense, money has little to do with whether or not

you're a good parent. It doesn't matter whether you have a lot of it or very little. It does matter, however, how much you're controlled by money. If you let it have too much power over you, either because of its presence or absence, you run the danger of inadvertently teaching your children that money is worth pursuing at the expense of other important values.

Teach your kids to respect money? Yes. Teach them that the only way to get money is to work for it? Yes. Teach them to be generous with it and honest about it? Yes. But also teach them that money is only a means, never an end in itself. Like all God's blessings, money is not really ours to keep for ourselves anyway. It's only ours to use, for God's purposes. So it's important, but not all-important. Good parents know that, and they pass that knowledge on to their kids.

· TWELVE ·

Give Your Children Responsibility

My parents were very strong in encouraging the notion that people got things because they worked for them. They instilled in me that people who work hard for a living for their kids and family are very admirable. I think their greatest strength as parents was giving me a sense of discipline and hard work, a sense that anything you got in life you had to earn.

Fred Barnes

I remember my mother saying over and over, "The best thing I can do for you as a mother is help you grow up and make decisions. One day you'll be on your own and be able to do that." I think she was very wise.

Janet Getz

ALTHOUGH IT'S BECOME A popular philosophy that childhood should be a protected time in which children are free from the worries and work of adults, it's been my observation that children who know they are needed, who know they have an important contribution to make to the family, develop a

187

strong sense of self-esteem as well as good habits that
contribute to later success.

The reverse also seems to be true. Grace Ketterman is a
pediatrician and child psychiatrist who has worked with
troubled kids for many years. One of the notable characteristics of the young people she works with, she says, is a
seriously deficient sense of responsibility. Many observers
believe lack of responsibility is a root cause of some of our
nation's most difficult problems—teenage pregnancy, the
high dropout rate in urban schools, overcrowded prisons, and
welfare dependency, for example.

While I would never advocate the sweatshop form of child
labor that existed in this country early in this century—and
still exists in many Third-World countries today—I've come
to believe that even a fairly heavy load of responsibility can be
healthy for a child. Some of our country's most successful
people sowed the seeds of their success during childhoods
that some might consider unnecessarily burdened by responsibility.

Take Mary Kay Ash, for example. As a child, she was
responsible for all the duties her mother would have performed had she been able to stay home. From the time she
was seven years old, Ash took care of the house and cooked
and took care of all her father's medical needs. "I got up early
in the morning and made breakfast for my dad and myself,"
she explains. "I'd see that he had whatever he needed before I
left for school; I'd put books or magazines or whatever he
needed on the table next to him. When I came home, I'd find
out what he wanted for supper, fix it, and then take care of the
house. The rest of the time I spent on my lessons. I was a
straight-A student, and I'd take whatever time was necessary
to have my lessons in perfect order for the next day. In
retrospect, I think my mother probably was thinking to
herself, *What am I putting on this little kid's shoulders?* But I
thought everybody did what I did. It was just my life."

Mary Kay Ash never resented the heavy load of responsibility she was given because she could see that her efforts were needed and because she respected the example set by her parents. "I never asked, Why me?" she says. "I loved my dad, I could see that my mother was working to take care of us, and what I was doing was just part of what needed to be done. Besides, my mother's attitude communicated itself to me. She worked so long and hard, and I appreciated that."

Under other circumstances, Ash's parents probably wouldn't have chosen to give her as much responsibility as she ended up having. But in giving her what many people might consider too much responsibility, they gave her a tremendous gift—a gift that contributed to her outstanding achievements in later life.

Wise parents do deliberately what Ash's parents did of necessity. They give their children the gift of responsibility, and in return they experience the joy of giving the world productive citizens: men and women who have a strong work ethic, who understand that effort precedes reward, who accept the consequences of their actions.

EARLY PRACTICE

Effective parents give their children opportunities to exercise responsibility beginning in early childhood, most often in the form of household chores. The types of chores my interviewees were given varied according to the setting in which the family lived, with farm kids getting perhaps the heaviest load of work. Elaine Kirk's memories are typical of interviewees who had a rural upbringing. "My parents believed in the work ethic," she observes. "We worked hard on the farm, and all of us helped out, whether in the field or the house or the garden. We had to milk cows, clean the horse barn, and feed the animals. We worked long hours in the fields. We had chickens all over the farm, and every night when we'd get home from school, we'd have to gather the eggs. One of my jobs was to get on my pony and fetch the cows for milking. We also picked strawberries. When it was strawberry season, the sun shone down and it was unbearably hot. I hated picking strawberries, but I did it."

While urban and suburban life doesn't seem to require as much physical labor as a farming existence, wise parents who live in the former settings know as well as their counterparts in the country that it's important for children to learn to pitch in. Like Terry Tochihara's family, they specify tasks—doing dishes, making beds, taking out the garbage, folding laundry, whatever is appropriate to the age of the child and the needs of the household—and make sure their children are clear about their responsibility for accomplishing them. "I had many girlfriends who never did dishes or cleaned the house because their mother did it," says Tochihara. "But in our family, that was our responsibility. We set up lists of whose turn it was to do things. We had responsibilities at an early age."

Often, good parents assign chores as a way of teaching their children the benefits of cooperation. When Jon Ebersole's family went camping, for example, "Everyone had a little task. I can still tell you what I did. I'd put the stakes down. We'd get to the campsite, and I'd put these stakes around. Each one of us had a job, and we did it."

BE CREATIVE

Good parents are strategic in the way they introduce their children to responsibility. If possible, for example, they respond to their kids' natural interest—as young children—in imitating them and doing things with them. They allow their children to participate with them in various tasks that, to young eyes, can look like fun. "I remember being so thrilled at age six to be allowed to fold towels and iron my dad's handkerchiefs," recalls Janet Getz. "I couldn't wait to iron the pillowcases! There was no reason to iron a pillowcase, but Mom was allowing me to do that because she knew I couldn't do other things."

Jon Ebersole has similar memories. "My parents included us in doing things with them when we were really little, so when we got older, it was a natural progression. Mom would pull a chair up so I could help make cookies or help dry the dishes, things like that. And I was always following my dad around, carrying a bucket for him or a rake for the garden. He would let me participate in what he was doing. It just made sense. The kid wanted to help, so they let the kid help—even though it took longer to get things done. But what happened was, as we got older, we just naturally did chores."

Good parents respond to their young children's natural interest in imitating them, even when it would be easier not to. Observes Getz, "My mom would be doing something like painting the house or my dad would be doing something like weeding the garden, and as little kids we would say, 'I can do this!' Some parents would think, *Oh, it's going to be a total mess!* But they invited us to participate."

ALTERNATIVES TO NAGGING

Effective parents know that nagging children to do their chores doesn't teach responsibility, it only creates a negative attitude. Instead of constant reminders, and punishment when their children "forget" to carry out a responsibility, these parents just quietly make sure their children follow through—as Grace Ketterman's parents did. "When I forgot my chores," she says, "my dad wouldn't just punish me and let me off the hook. He made me do the job, which helped me remember more than constant reminders would have. Constant nagging, rather than teaching a child responsibility, creates negativism. The children who 'forget' are in a bind.

They want to please, but they also want to be free to do their own thing. I learned that you do the job and you don't feel guilty."

Because their mother was always out working to support them, Benjamin Carson and his brother were responsible for doing virtually all the household chores in their family. But like most children, they had a tendency to "forget." When Mrs. Carson got tired of nagging her sons to do their chores, instead of taking on those jobs herself, she let the boys come up with a plan for getting them done on their own. "She basically left it up to my brother and me to figure out how to get things done," recalls Carson. "She said, 'Why don't you guys decide what needs to be done, write it down, and then assign yourselves appropriate jobs.' When we had to write it down ourselves, we couldn't say 'Somebody else made this rule.' So it worked really well."

WORK TOWARD BALANCE

Good parents know it's important to balance responsibility with free time for a child to pursue his or her own interests. Mary Kay Ash recalls that, despite her many household responsibilities as a young girl, she still spent a lot of time playing with neighborhood children. She even participated in holiday activities and took vacations with her friend Dorothy. And, although Gregg Roeber's parents have sometimes wondered if perhaps they gave him too much responsibility as a child, he remembers that they always gave him enough time off from his work on their Colorado ranch to pursue his recreational interests. "There was always more work to be done than anybody could have done," he says, "and many children who grew up on those ranches were put to severe work at a very early age. That wasn't the case with me. My parents gave me chores to do, but they had an interest in and a respect for learning. Both my parents allowed me to do a great deal of reading, for example. And when I heard my mother playing the piano and said I wanted to learn, I was allowed to take lessons."

WORKING FOR LOVE AND MONEY

Many children of good parents say that doing household chores helped teach them responsibility because they were doing them to contribute to the welfare of the entire family, not because they got paid. "The jobs we did—washing up, keeping our rooms clean, working together as a family—those were just things we did as part of the family," says Janet Getz. "A lot of families say, 'You get paid for doing that.' We didn't. It was more like, 'You're part of us, and this is what we do.'"

Julie Ravencroft recalls, "The kids across the street would always get money from their parents if they did things like rake the leaves. But my parents' line was, 'In this house, we do things for love.' Of course, when you're a kid, that's not the way it works!" she laughs. "But when I look back, I think that was a real important value."

There's nothing wrong with teaching kids to work for money, however. In fact, many children of good parents say their parents encouraged them to find ways to earn their own money, and as a consequence, they learned at an early age that hard work can bring satisfying rewards.

Take Jay Kesler, for example. One of the characteristics he appreciates most about his parents is the fact that they encouraged industry. "We always had a little business," Kesler recalls. "Sometimes we'd have a lemonade stand. And in front of our house we had a sign announcing that I sold crickets and redworms. I would catch crickets and find redworms in the park and then sell them for 25 cents a hundred. My parents always let me have that dumb little sign in the yard. We were always coming up with enterprising ideas, and my dad would go over our profits with us. I had a job from the time I was twelve. I delivered papers, sacked groceries, whatever. We were raised with the idea that those who don't work, don't eat."

Louis McBurney says that because his parents encouraged him rather than forced him to work, it seemed like a privilege. "I was ten or eleven when I got my first summer and weekend job, and I really enjoyed having my own money," he recalls. "My first job was stocking shelves and cleaning up at a children's clothing store. After that, I worked summers where my dad worked. He was an ice-cream salesperson, and I would work on an ice-cream truck, delivering ice cream all over that part of the state. I was probably twelve when the driver would let me drive the truck between towns. It was terribly illegal, but fun. Then I worked for a dry-cleaning business. When Dad got out of the ice-cream business and bought a little convenience store, I worked there in the evenings and weekends. In the summers, Dad would let me run the store. He would pretty much take off from the time I was a junior in high school. I was writing checks for other employees and all that kind of stuff. It was really good experience."

CAN KIDS LEARN RESPONSIBILITY WITHOUT CHORES?

Giving kids household chores and encouraging them to earn their own money from outside jobs are time-honored tactics for teaching responsibility. But to my great surprise, many adult children attested to the fact that it's possible to raise responsible kids without doing either. Nancy Swider-Peltz is a case in point.

Swider-Peltz is a four-time Olympic athlete, a speedskater and former 3000-meter world-record holder. Now a mother of two, Swider-Peltz still coaches and is considering a competitive comeback. Qualifying for the Olympics once, let alone four times, takes incredible grit, determination, and discipline—all of which this outstanding athlete has. She credits her parents with developing these traits in her. But while she was growing up, Swider-Peltz had virtually no regular household responsibilities. The same was true of her brothers. So how is it that she and her siblings grew up to be so responsible?

Even she can't figure it out.

"It baffles me," she says. "My two brothers and I are excessively meticulous, we keep immaculate houses, but we never had consistent chores to do around the house. We never had jobs like taking out the garbage or making the beds, at least not as a consistent thing. I remember not making my bed for weeks because I was so busy with sports and academics and church. My mom would sometimes ask me to make cookies or get my bedroom cleaned, but it was never a permanent job. People often thought that was horrible, that we would never learn to be neat, responsible people. But the opposite happened."

After pondering Swider-Peltz's experience for a while, I've come up with two explanations for how she and her brothers turned out the way they did. First, even though they didn't have to do any regular household chores, she and her siblings did have responsibilities. They were required to give their all to schoolwork, church, and any extracurricular activities they chose to participate in. They were encouraged to pursue their interests, but they were also required to take responsibility for their choices. "We could choose any activity we wanted," says Swider-Peltz, "but there were two rules: we could never miss a practice, and we could never quit."

Swider-Peltz's parents also modeled a strong sense of responsibility and a strong work ethic. Her father was a gifted athlete and coach, whose leadership skills could have taken him far beyond his teaching position at the local high school.

But he stayed there because he was determined to spend time with his family. He saved all the money he made from coaching—which he considered 'extra' money even though his teacher's salary was modest—and put it into college funds for his kids. Swider-Peltz's mother worked as a substitute teacher to help support the family. Swider-Peltz's mom and dad both were willing to do most of the household chores so their children would be free to pursue what the parents felt were more important activities. "Our parents sacrificed so we could achieve in other areas," Swider-Peltz says, "but I don't think we ever thought we were too good to clean the toilet. I clean toilets all the time now!"

Modeling responsibility and a strong work ethic appears to be one of the secrets of raising responsible children. Making your kids do chores or get a job is of minimum value if you don't show them what responsibility and hard work look like in adult life. Ron Hutchcraft recalls, "My dad really inspired me by modeling a great work ethic. He taught that it's good to work hard. He was a very industrious man. One reason he overachieved—everybody else who was at his level in his company was a college graduate—was the fact that what he lacked in education, he seemed to make up in character. He was very industrious and hardworking, and I think that rubbed off on me."

The Power of a Good Example

When children see their parents working hard and behaving responsibly, it seems to make such a strong impression that these children are likely to imitate their parents in adulthood. Doug Anderson is a good example.

Doug is a respected neurosurgeon. At least that's what he does professionally. He's also an acclaimed vocalist who has sung at the White House and who could have had a successful career as an opera singer. He was offered college scholarships in both music and gymnastics and was a serious Olympic contender. He's an accomplished tennis player, sailor, and skier, and he can hold his own in serious theological discussions. In short, Anderson is an overachiever. But, he says, the discipline and hard work and sense of responsibility that have helped him become an overachiever came more from his observation of his parents than from his childhood training.

"Unfortunately, I was a little bit spoiled in that, if I didn't clean my room, my mom would clean it," he says. "If I didn't make my bed, she'd make it. She was always willing to do that. Every once in a while my parents would zap me, though. All my friends would be going to the Tastee Freeze, and my parents would ask, 'Did you cut the grass as we asked you?' 'No, but I can do it as soon as I get back.' 'No, you've got to do it now.' That made it clear to me that they weren't fooling around. But when it comes down to it, what really sunk in was their example more than their method of teaching me.

"I was always aware of my father's work ethic," Anderson continues. "He was famous among all the family. The family knew him as this guy who started his own business at the age of twelve and then sold it in high school to his elder sister's husband, who ran it for the rest of his life! He had a huge business, and everybody was impressed by that. He was driving a nice car to high school in the forties—the only kid around who had a beautiful new car—because he had his own business. His work ethic was obviously pretty intense."

While I don't recommend making your kids' beds for them—particularly if it's an assigned task—Anderson's story is strong evidence that modeling can sometimes be just as important as early training in developing a sense of responsibility in children.

WORK WITH YOUR KIDS

One of the most effective ways to model responsibility for your kids is to include them in your work. "I think my mom and dad's genius was the fact that they brought us in on their work," says Judy Anderson of her missionary parents. "We felt we were part of it. Even if we were just entertaining guests or showing people around the city where we lived, we felt we were part of what they were doing."

Children of good parents say there is a big difference between being sent off to do a job and being invited to work together on a job. "We were invited to participate in doing things around the house as opposed to being told to do things," observes Janet Getz.

Children of good parents likewise observe that tasks take on a new significance when they're shared with adults. As a young boy growing up on a farm, Richard Chase's chores weren't just chores; they were important jobs because they were part of his dad's work. "Since we lived on the farm," he says, "Dad's work was right there. He'd go out in the morning to do chores, and we'd tag along, and before long our task was to feed the calves and work on the machinery. I can remember working in the machine shop, working on trucks, and so forth. We thought it was a lot of work, and we had to do it. But Dad was there helping, and we got lots of experience."

TEACHING PRACTICAL LIFE SKILLS

The experience that Dick Chase got working on the farm, he believes, gave him some life skills that have served him well as an adult. He no longer needs to use his knowledge about doctoring a sick cow, but the sense of competence he got from doing that at a young age has helped him throughout his life.

Teaching children life skills, as Dick Chase's parents did, is an important component of teaching them to be responsible. Janet Getz says it was one of her parents' great strengths. "I can remember talking with peers who said, 'Oh, I had to learn to cook when I got married,' or something along those lines," she recalls. "But we were able to help from the time I was really small. A friend of mine from grade school told me once, 'I remember coming to your house in second grade, and you fixed lunch. I was stunned, but I thought, *I wish I could do this.*' My mom let us bake cakes and cookies and help her with parties. She taught us to serve things and how to make dishes look nice. Dad helped us learn how to do gardening. We always had animals to take care of and many different pets. We had to make sure the animals were fed and cared for and cleaned. So we learned to be responsible."

LET THEM TRY THEIR WINGS

To be useful, life skills have to be tested under real life conditions. So wise parents give their children increasing opportunities to exercise both their skills and their judgment as they get older. They encourage ever-increasing degrees of independence. And they allow their children to take considered risks.

Janet Getz says her parents were especially good at encouraging her and her sisters to develop their decision-making skills. "My mom was very wise in preparing us to grow up and leave home," reflects Getz. "She would say things like, 'It's important that you try this or that you make this decision. It's right and good that you should grow up and be able to do this.' Obviously there are times when it's hard to do. It's so easy to say, 'Wait. Stop. I want you back!' But we saw my parents taking risks and allowing us to take risks. They were willing to take the risk of going overseas to live, of starting over time and time again. They let my sister go to

Russia when she was in only ninth grade. When we lived in England, they let my other sister go to Yorkshire for a two-week work trip on a farm when she was in seventh grade. They encouraged us to try things, even when they were above and beyond us."

Grace Ketterman went to high school during World War II, when gas was rationed. Since it was impossible to drive to school from their farm, fifteen-year-old Ketterman and her seventeen-year-old sister lived away from home in an apartment. "We both got part-time jobs, took care of ourselves, and were very nearly self-supporting," explains Ketterman. "The kind of independence that experience demanded and the trust my parents gave us is absolutely incredible to me. It gave me a real boost in self-confidence to know that I could do it. I could be responsible to get my homework done. I could clean the house, get my clothes done. When I went away to college, I had no doubts that I would be able to handle my life. And I felt good about it." In giving their daughter an unusual degree of independence, Ketterman's parents encouraged some important character qualities that have helped her throughout her life.

Gretchen Ziegenhals's parents were undoubtedly concerned about some of the risks she took as a young woman, but they trusted her and knew that allowing basically responsible children to take a certain degree of considered risk can build character. "I think my parents were probably very nervous about some of the risks I've taken, but they never said it," observes Ziegenhals. "I went to Vienna for my junior year of college, for example, and traveled around Europe by myself first. When I think about it now, I don't know if I'd do it again. Obviously, my parents hoped they had taught me how to handle myself, but there was a safety factor for a young college woman to do that. Even deciding to stay on the East Coast and work after college instead of coming home to the Midwest, I think that was engendered by a sense of independence my parents fostered in me. I could go anywhere in the country I wanted for a job, and it was an adventure."

THE GIFT OF TRUST

Here is yet another irony: parents give their children the gift of trust when they see their kids are responsible. On the other hand, children tend to become responsible when they are trusted. Good parents do everything they can to produce responsible children—and then let them know they trust them. "I was trusted enormously," says Steve Roskam of his upbringing. "My parents put me on a plane and let me live in Europe for a year by myself when I was seventeen. I went alone from Illinois to Colorado by train when I was thirteen to go to camp. My parents would leave me to baby-sit the younger kids. I felt they had enormous trust in me, and even though I violated the trust sometimes, I ultimately lived up to it. If people trust you, you become trustworthy."

Having raised her to be responsible, O'Ann Steere's parents trusted her under circumstances that would have tested the discipline of most parents. "Every time we went out the door, we always had a quarter in our shoe or a dime in our pocket," explains Steere. "My dad said, 'If you ever need me, you can call home.' Well, I got myself in a bad situation once. I was embarrassed about it—I knew I wasn't in a good situation— but I called my parents and said, 'This is the address. Come and get me.' My dad picked me up, and even though my blouse was ripped down to the waist, he never said a word except, 'You need a new dime.' I've since realized what a staggering amount of trust and self-control that took. To this day, my parents must wonder what happened, but they spared me a lecture about something I already knew. They promised they would pick us up when we were in trouble, and they did. And they didn't get involved in the situation."

UNDERSTANDING CONSEQUENCES

Responsible kids differ from irresponsible kids in essentially one way: responsible kids understand the law of cause and effect. They believe that their actions have consequences. If they contribute to the well-being of the larger family by doing their household chores, they earn the privileges of being part of the family community. If they get a job and work hard, they can enjoy the freedoms that go along with earning their own money. If they are diligent about their schoolwork and extracurricular activities, they earn the rewards that usually follow achievement.

Good parents let their children know that, while it might not seem like it early on, life is a lot easier and much more rewarding when you work with the law of cause and effect instead of against it. As Judy Anderson says, "One of the best things parents can do is teach their children that they're responsible for themselves, that their little choices add up."

Taking Responsibility for Others

Good parents also teach their children, as O'Ann Steere's parents did, that sometimes they need to be responsible not just for themselves but also for others. "We were fairly well off, and I remember my dad used to offer camp scholarships to kids who couldn't afford to go to camp—even though we had to earn half our own way. So we said, 'Wait a minute! You're going to send other kids free, and we have to earn half our way?' The response was, 'Yes. I'll help you find work. I'll teach you to work. But if you want to go to camp, you have to work.' I think this was a wonderful approach. We recognized that some parents couldn't pay the other half. But my parents helped us find work. Today, I'm pretty glad they taught me to work. Some people in the world need a handout, but by the grace of God, I'm one of the people who needs to be working hard and handing out."

As the head of pediatric neurosurgery at Johns Hopkins Hospital, Benjamin Carson wants to know what's happening with each patient in his department, even those assigned to other doctors. If something were to go wrong, he would hold himself responsible. There would be no excuses—that's how he was raised.

"In my mother's book," he explains, "there was no such thing as a good excuse. Even if someone else was partially at fault, she would say, 'But you should have been able to assist the situation. You should have realized that person wasn't going to come through.' She always felt you should have been able to circumvent some unfortunate outcome. She would quote this poem called 'Yourself to Blame.' The bottom line was the idea that you're the captain of your ship. No matter what stormy seas you come across, you're the one who's steering. That's something I took to heart and still take to heart today. I always feel responsible for what happens with any patient on my service. Regardless of who's been assigned to do what, I want to know what's going on, and I do what's necessary to make sure there aren't problems."

By the grace of God, you can raise children who take responsibility for themselves and for others, who work hard, who accept the consequences of their choices, who understand the law of cause and effect, who know they are needed, who know they have a contribution to make. Such children tend to have a strong sense of self-esteem and, more often than not, good parents.

Be a good parent. Teach your kids responsibility.

· THIRTEEN ·

Have a Passionate Agenda

> *My parents had very strong opinions: about premarital sex as being wrong, about abortion being murder, about us all being equal even though some people are prejudiced against blacks or others. As a teenager, I didn't always want to hear these things, but as I got older, I started to appreciate that my parents had some really strong stands on things.*
>
> Julie Ravencroft
>
> *Taking a stand on things was very important to my parents. My dad would stand up for what he believed in at work. He was an example of someone who could be a nice guy in a business setting, a nice guy who could finish first.*
>
> Molly Cline

BRENDA WATKINS HAS VIVID memories of the discussions she and her brother Calvin used to have with their father, pastor of an African-American church in San Francisco. They would talk about spirituality, about racial issues, about injustice in the world. Sometimes they would talk late into the night, alternately listening and arguing for passionately held views. "Things related to the faith or to the black community were very near and dear to my dad," Watkins recalls, "and he had very strong opinions. Sometimes when we got into these heated discussions of issues and situations, my dad would cry. Some things just touched him in a very deep way, and that's how it would come out. He would just be overcome.

"My parents had an agenda," Watkins continues. "They had a passion about community, about the Christian life. Somehow my dad felt as if everything he did made a difference. He didn't necessarily feel he was so important. But there was work to be done! There were people out there, things to do, needs to be met! Somehow he always felt God has called us to do some things. Most of what my father did revolved around that.

"My parents were very concerned that we not lose our perspective and lose our respect for the community and the people in the community. We went off to Harvard and Oxford; that's great. But we had to be able to relate and we had to be able to give and to serve. That was crucial.

"My dad had a funny saying. He said he didn't want us to grow up to be educated fools. He wanted us to be wise, to be sensitive, to be educated, to be caring, to be loving, to respect the church, to love God. Those were the things that were important."

Like Brenda Watkins' father, good parents teach their kids what's important. They have integrity, principles, values. They have a positive agenda—and they're passionate about it. They take stands. They do good. And they raise kids who not only know what's important but also have enormous respect for their parents.

INTEGRITY

When I asked Madeleine L'Engle what she appreciated most about her parents, her first response was, "They were people of integrity." Honesty and integrity seem to be important to most good parents. Many of the grown children I spoke with mentioned it. Like Joan Beck, whose father was CEO of a food company, the largest employer in their Iowa town. "I remember when I was in the third grade, everyone in my class had a mechanical pencil with the name of my father's company on it," Beck recalls. "I was the only one who didn't. But my father would no more think of bringing me a pencil from the company than of shooting somebody. You just didn't do that."

A POSITIVE AGENDA

Good parents have informed opinions. They've gone to the trouble of thinking about what they believe. They have a road map for getting through life, a road map based on values and principles.

As a middle-class white man living in a quiet town in Indiana, David Handley's father had no vested interest in the Civil Rights movement, but he somehow caught the vision of fighting for racial justice, and he became determined to pass that vision on to his kids. "My dad gave me the sense we should do something that made a difference in the world," observes Handley.

"I grew up in the civil-rights era, the late fifties and early sixties, and Martin Luther King, Jr., was a real controversy in our home town in Indiana. Our family was divided. My uncle thought Martin Luther King, Jr., was the biggest manipulator who ever lived. My dad would always defend King and was all for civil rights. He took me into Chicago when I was about ten when Martin Luther King, Jr., spoke to the Chicago Sunday Evening Club, which then met at Orchestra Hall. The place was packed. We were probably five out of maybe a hundred white people in the whole place. There was so much black pride there. That made a profound impact on me. My father was very smart in giving us experiences like that, even when it was very inconvenient, like driving all the way into Chicago for that one event. He was very intentional."

Like David Handley's father, Louis McBurney's parents had no obvious predisposing reasons for their strong emphasis on respecting people regardless of their color or background. In fact, given the time and place in which they lived—the South during the segregation era—it would have been understandable if they had been less enlightened on the subject of racial equality. But they were firm in their belief in the inherent value of all humans, regardless of race. "Even though we grew up in the South when segregation was still in effect in all public facilities and blacks all lived in one part of town," muses McBurney, "we were always taught by both my parents to respect all people. I got two kinds of messages: one, that I wasn't better than anybody else, no matter what color or station in life the other person was; and two, that I was just as good as anybody else, that I could feel at ease around princes or paupers."

Gretchen Ziegenhals's parents were determined that she and her brother learn to understand and get along with people not only from different races but also from different ethnic, religious, and economic backgrounds. "I can remember having many family conversations about how people ticked and about how to respect different kinds of people and how to recognize the good in people we didn't necessarily like and didn't necessarily understand," recalls Ziegenhals. "I can remember that from my very earliest days. My father also instilled a respect for the working class, for blue-collar workers. That was a real value on his part. He felt that summer jobs were very important for understanding a variety of work experiences. He and my mother helped us find jobs that would earn a little money and yet expose us to different kinds of people."

PRINCIPLES THAT TRANSLATE INTO ACTION

Good parents' principles don't exist in a vacuum. Rather, these men and women have principles that guide their lives, principles that are lived out in front of their kids. Julie Ravencroft's parents, for example, had a commitment to justice and compassion for the poor, a commitment that shaped their entire family life. The parents of four biological children, the Ravencrofts adopted two additional children—one African-American and one Chinese—and took in countless foster children. This very concrete approach to acting on their concern for others has had a significant effect on Ravencroft and has given her some vivid memories.

"I remember we went to pick up two foster brothers who were living in Cabrini Green (a low-income housing project known for extreme poverty and violence) right after the Chicago riots in 1968," Ravencroft says. "Here's this white family going up the elevator. The whole family went. We were little, but with Mom and Dad we felt safe. I'm not sure it was all that safe, but it probably wasn't as bad as it is now with all the drug stuff. My parents were concerned, but we went as a family. I think my parents thought, *The Lord is with us. We've got to do this, and we're going to do it.* I remember going with my mom a couple of other times to pick up a foster child. Going into old apartment buildings where it would smell like urine, my mom would say it was because the landlord didn't fix the elevators and the poor little kids couldn't get upstairs in time to go to the bathroom."

Nancy Swider-Peltz continues to be awed by the principles of sacrifice and selflessness by which her father lived. "I don't think you could find a more selfless individual than my dad," she says. "He had very strong desires for success and winning, but he put down his own ambitions to be somebody in this world for the sake of his kids and the sake of his students. As a coach, he wanted kids to learn important lessons in life through football. He felt the purpose of football in high school was not so much to win but to learn practical life lessons. If that meant sacrificing winning the game, he had to sacrifice his desire to win for the betterment of the individuals on the team. The same with his kids. He truly wanted us to do well and to win because he felt that would teach us something we could use in life. But I never felt it was for him personally. I'm extremely respecting of that. I wish I could be as selfless as my dad. I've never met anybody like him."

Sometimes, living out deeply held principles means taking a stand. And count on it, children remember when their parents stand on principle. Nancy Tecson, for example, desperately wanted her parents to join their local tennis club so she could use the pool. But she respects her father to this day for refusing to join because, at the time, the club discriminated against Catholics and Jews.

Jay Kesler has indelible memories of his father, a blue-collar factory worker, championing the underdog as a local leader in the labor movement. "My father was always embroiled in controversy," says Kesler, "always working on behalf of poor people, always trying to get better wages for the black workers in the plant, that kind of thing. The community we lived in was quite a conservative community, and his politics tended to be more liberal than most of the kids' dads. So I was always wearing the wrong button when it came election time. As a little boy in an almost totally Republican world, I was wearing a Roosevelt button."

Brenda Watkins will never forget one particular time her father took a stand on principle—don't buy into the world's standards—because it was her behavior that prompted the incident. "When I came back home after my first year of college," she recalls, "I had a very hard time relating to my mom. My mom was older, so I felt as if she didn't have the energy to do a lot of the things my friends' moms did. And I did a lot of comparing. One time I said something disrespectful, and my dad chastised me very strongly. He made me apologize to my mother. It was clear: <u>you don't ever</u> <u>disrespect</u>; you don't disrespect the family; you don't disrespect the community. There was a perspective that <u>we cannot</u> <u>buy into the world's definition of who we are</u>. That was unacceptable. It was dehumanizing to many people who haven't had the opportunities we have had. No matter how many little airs I had, my parents kept bringing that message home. They taught me what was important. And I appreciate that to this day."

DOING GOOD

Sometimes living by principle is less dramatic than taking a stand. Sometimes it means living quietly and doing good, not just avoiding evil, but taking positive steps to help others, to make the world a better place.

Luis Palau's parents didn't make a big commotion about it, but as far back as he can remember, they taught him and his siblings to care for people less fortunate than they themselves were. "We were always encouraged to think of helping the widows and orphans," he recalls. "From my youngest childhood I remember that mindset, that the widows and orphans must be cared for at any sacrifice or cost. As a result, even when I was a teenager I would go with friends of mine to a house deeded to some widows. It was a very poor situation, and we would go on Saturdays and take food, clothing, wood for the fireplace. We had Bible studies and sang and took whatever pennies we could take. When my dad was alive, we were well off, but three years later, we were pretty much in poverty ourselves. Yet we never thought, *Hey, I don't have that much myself, somebody else will have to take care of these people.* There was a total commitment to caring for widows and orphans."

Luis Palau is not alone in his memories of a childhood

emphasis on doing good. <u>Grown children of good parents</u> <u>repeatedly spoke of how significant it was for them to observe</u> <u>their parents reaching out to others with a spirit of compas-</u> <u>sion and generosity.</u>

David Heim's parents were deeply involved in their community's school and childcare issues. They helped resettle refugees. They went to Central America on a teaching mission, and Heim's father took time out from his pastorate to serve as chaplain on the ship *Hope*.

Nancy Tecson's parents lived a quiet life of concern for others. Her mother volunteered for the Cancer Society, visited people in the hospital, made meals for people going through hard times. Her father was always quick to respond to a need by mowing someone's lawn or fixing an air conditioner. They both made it a priority to visit elderly people who didn't have anyone else to come see them. "Even then," says Tecson, "I noticed the way my dad would walk down the hall of a nursing home and go into a room to talk to the older women who were just sitting there all day."

Mary O'Connor's parents opened their home to pregnant teenage girls, and on one occasion a great-aunt who had no place to live ended up staying with them for seven years. "There was no grumbling," notes O'Connor. "They just took her in."

Good parents don't waste <u>time warning their children</u> <u>about what they shouldn't do because they're too busy</u> <u>modeling what they *should* do</u>. Like Timothy Johnson's mother and father. An active deaconess in the church, his mother was always calling on people, doing them favors, bringing them food in times of need. And even though he didn't have a lot, Johnson's father was notably generous in his giving to causes like the Salvation Army and in his assistance to needy people, like the impoverished young church member he helped go to college.

Dick Chase's parents were so generous in sharing with

others that they had very few resources left in their old age. "They basically shared with anybody and everybody," recalls Chase. "We lived right by a railroad track, and during the Depression, hobos would come to the door. Mom would say, 'If you mow the lawn, I'll pack you a lunch.' Sometimes the work they did was almost insignificant, but Mom would pack them a great big sack lunch. Anybody and everybody who came by would get help from my parents."

As farmers, Grace Ketterman's parents had much food even during the Depression, and families who came to visit them rarely left without taking some produce or a dozen eggs. And her parents always seemed to be taking people in. "Very often somebody who was unfortunate and needed a home for a while lived with us," recalls Ketterman. "Missionaries who needed a place to stay, visiting ministers, people connected to the church, they were all guests in our home. It certainly enriched my life and taught me to be generous and caring."

Learning Through Participation

Wise parents know that children learn from doing. So David Handley's father, for example, was very intentional about taking his children with him when he delivered turkey dinners to poor families at Christmas time. Effective parents give their children opportunities to participate with them in reaching out to others, as Melinda Schmidt's mother did. "We lived at a busy corner, where there were many accidents," explains Schmidt. "Whenever we would hear an accident, Mom would say, 'Okay, kids, go get the lawn chairs.' So here would be a little five-year-old and eight-year-old, traipsing down to this busy road with lawn chairs to take to the people who were in an accident. My mom would witness to them and pray for them, and we were there to make them comfortable until the ambulance came. That's how my mom is."

OPENNESS TO SERVICE

Like Melinda Schmidt's mother, good parents seem to have an unusual capacity to see opportunities for service. Steve Roskam's father, for example, was reading a magazine on a plane when he got an idea for how to help young people get an education. "He was reading a *Time* magazine article about a bartering company that would acquire different materials for people and barter back and forth," explains Roskam, "and out of that, he developed a concept to help kids go to college. Basically he went around and acquired slow-moving materials—backed-up inventory from various corporations. He'd get them a tax write-off and take that material and go to colleges. For instance, he would go to a desk company and ask for desks to donate and then go to a university that needed desks and give them to the school and charge them a ten-percent fee. The other ninety percent of equivalent funds go to finance kids who wouldn't otherwise be able to go to college. He's been doing that six or seven years now. They have about five or six million dollars in scholarships they've generated every year."

SUPPORTING KIDS' COMPASSIONATE INITIATIVE

Good parents are supportive when their children show initiative in reaching out with compassion. When O'Ann Steere's sister invited a schoolmate, a victim of abuse and neglect, to come to live with her, for example, Steere's parents didn't blink an eyelash. "My sister sat next to this girl in school and found out she was going to have to leave because her mother was put in a state mental hospital and her dad had hit her, knocking her out cold on the sidewalk," explains Steere. "He had smashed her head and thrown her down. My sister said, 'Well, you can come to live with us.' So we went and picked her up and moved her into our house for a couple of days. I remember my dad coming home from work. He said, 'The more the merrier.' There was no social-work inquisition or 'What is she doing here?' She stayed with us for two weeks, and then we went through the process of formalizing things. She became our foster sister."

BALANCE

I couldn't help but wonder whether, in the midst of all this "doing good," these parents' kids sometimes felt they were getting the short end of the stick. Did they ever feel their parents were spending so much time helping other people that they neglected their own families?

Few of the grown children I talked with seemed to feel this way. By definition, good parents are committed to the good of their own families as well as the good of the rest of the world. Brenda Watkins reflects on her civic-minded, ministry-oriented father: "Because my dad was able to go to my Halloween parade, able to go and root for Calvin at the football game, he could still be present for us. He didn't lift his community involvement above us as individuals. I think he gave us a healthy perspective and balance. Many of the things he was involved with were important, but out of balance they might have caused other difficulties. I think my dad tried to come up with a healthy balance, and I think he did a fairly good job."

Like so many other things in life, living out one's principles in the world has to be done in a balanced way. Children are among the prime beneficiaries when parents have a positive agenda based on integrity and principles. They learn important lessons when they see their parents taking a stand, pursuing passionate ideals, and doing good in a quiet and consistent way. Some of the most effective parents are those who have a strong agenda based on positive values, especially spiritually based values, who reach out to others in pursuit of that agenda, and who don't forget that their own kids need them as much as anyone else in the world.

• FOURTEEN •

Put It All Together

IF YOU'VE READ THIS FAR, you may be thinking about the characteristics of good parents from two different perspectives. You may be thinking about these traits from the viewpoint of an adult child who is still processing and evaluating your own upbringing. Or you may be thinking about them from the viewpoint of a parent who is struggling to do your best to raise your children.

If you're comparing yourself to the parents described in these pages, you may feel either challenged or discouraged. Listening to stories about unusually effective parents can challenge us to emulate their characteristics and become better parents ourselves, or it can discourage us because we feel as if we've got such a long way to go.

I had both reactions as I listened to the recollections and reflections of grown children of good parents. Sometimes I was exhilarated: "Yes. That's it! This is the key!" Other times, I was completely deflated, overcome by the evidence of my parental deficiencies and failures.

If you're like me, the responsibility of parenting feels pretty heavy much of the time. My worrier self says: I'm doing my best, but what if I mess up? What if I'm not encouraging enough? What if my kids don't perceive the love I try to show them? What if I'm not consistent enough or reasonable enough in my discipline? What if I'm not part of—and can't find—a warm and nurturing community to help make my kids feel safe and reinforce my values? What if I don't spend enough time with them or enough of the right kind of time? What if I fail to make them proud of me? What if they reject the values I try to teach them? What if my husband and I develop marital problems or go through difficult times that we find impossible to face with a smile?

What if I try my hardest to do everything right, and my kids still go wrong?

It's possible. No parent or set of parents is perfect, and it's all too easy to use parental imperfection as an excuse for wrong choices and unhealthy behavior. As children grow into adults, they have a choice: they can build on their parents' strengths and forgive them for their weaknesses, or they can take the strengths for granted and focus on the weaknesses.

Which brings me to the second perspective from which to read this book—the perspective of an adult child whose parents weren't perfect. It would be easy to read a book of stories about good parents and to make negative comparisons with your own parents. It would be easy to view yourself as a victim because your parents didn't encourage you or tell you they loved you or make you feel safe or whatever. It would be easy to excuse yourself for your own failings because your parents had failings too.

It was interesting that virtually all the grown children I interviewed were careful to point out that their parents had flaws, in some cases, glaring flaws. And several interviewees confided that they had siblings who were much less appreciative of their parents than they themselves were.

Can parents with lots of weaknesses be "good" parents? The answer, I believe, is yes.

I was amazed, in talking with grown children who appreciated their parents, at how a few strengths can overshadow many perceived weaknesses. A man said to me recently, "You know, as strict as I thought my dad was and as much as I butted heads with him sometimes, I always knew that he had a tender heart for me. And that went a long way." Many other grown children have said something similar. Apparently, the knowledge that your parents deeply care for you and truly want the best for you can make up for many technical errors in childrearing.

I was also fascinated by what appears to be the conscious choice of some adults to see and appreciate the good in the parents they were given. I think that may be one explanation for why two children of the same parents can view them entirely differently. As the saying goes, some people prefer to see the glass as half-full; others see it as half-empty.

When I finished my interview with author Madeleine L'Engle, I turned off my tape recorder and started mumbling pleasantries in preparation to go on my way. But before I could leave, she leaned over and switched the recorder back on. "I'm very happy that you are writing a book about positive parenting," she said. "I am so tired of blaming parents for everything, and I think this is going to be an important book." And then she switched it back off.

Madeleine L'Engle, like all children of human parents, did not grow up in a perfect family. Her parents chose to raise her in an apartment in New York City, to go out almost every night to the opera or theater, to let her eat her meals alone in her room, to send her to a school where she was picked on and where she felt like a clumsy failure. But instead of brooding on what some people might view as a lonely, even eccentric childhood, Madeleine chooses to celebrate the gifts her parents gave her: unconditional love, encouragement, a positive view of God, a passion for books, appreciation for art, a tradition of storytelling, exposure to the larger world. "I'm very much against this dumping-on-your-parents syndrome," says L'Engle. "The people who belong to various organizations that dump on their parents are asking for something that went away when Adam and Eve left the Garden. They have unrealistic expectations. <u>I could dump on my parents if I wanted to, but how silly! Where would my free will be then?</u>"

At one point in his life Harold Best, dean of the Wheaton College Conservatory of Music, very consciously decided to exercise his free will by acknowledging the good influence his parents had on him, forgiving the bad, and taking responsibility for himself. A pastor's son, Best grew up knowing that his parents were sincere in their love of him and the Lord, but he resents what he viewed as his father's self-centeredness and his mother's extreme fearfulness. Listen to his story as he tells it:

"Dad and Mom were in ministry with the Christian and Missionary Alliance. Dad was the son of a factory worker, and he quit school in the eighth grade to help the family. He married my mom, his next-door neighbor, when he was nineteen and she was eighteen. My dad came to know the Lord largely through my mother's witness, and they then went to what was formerly called the Missionary Training Institute and is now Nyack College. Somehow my dad got accepted with his eighth-grade education. After graduating, they proceeded into a series of different pastorates, and we moved a lot.

"Dad was kind of an intellectual grammarian—a measurer who was into data and factuality—while Mother was more of an intellectual poet. Mother was a very deep, very fearful lady. She was raised with a strong Holiness theology, which made her afraid a lot. She was afraid of sinning away the day of grace, of not pleasing the Lord. Dad was more inclined to say, 'Well, this is what the Scriptures say.' He didn't really enter into the speculative side of things. But he was a deeply needy man because he felt himself to be inferior. Dad didn't know it and he didn't mean to be, but he was sort of a narcissist. He needed constant support, encouragement, and attention.

"The thing that really got to me about my dad was his continual adoration of me. I was his credential. When I was very young, my dad saw I was talented, and I became his alter ego, almost to the point that I felt he worshiped me. I'm an organist, and my dad just loved the organ, and he loved to hear me play. He bragged about me being a concert organist even though I wasn't. But my achievements built him up. I could just smell it. My sister felt it too. She and I have shared some very deep things in recent years, and I now realize that she was somewhat overlooked because of me.

"In any case, I went through a period of rebellion. I really went off the deep end in my high school years, but I was able to hide it from my parents until one night after a party. My friends and I had gone to someone's house and gotten half-loaded and did some damage to the house. Everybody got put in jail except me. The other kids didn't give the cops my name because they wanted to protect the preacher's kid. But finally my name came out. So the sheriff came by the house the next day to talk to me. I was in the bathroom, trying to get halfway sober, and he called me out, and said in front of my mom, 'Harold, where are you getting all the booze you're drinking?' And my mother, with her tender, tender, poetic, fearful, Holiness conscience, just came unglued. That's when they found out about me.

"After that I had a series of what I would call transitory, experimental repentances and backslidings. It wasn't until after college and several years of slow maturing, that the Lord really met me, and I mean really met me, when I was about thirty. By that time I had taught four years in a Christian college out East and was doing well. But I knew I needed to go deeper with the Lord. So I prayed deeply to him one day to bring me to him whatever it cost. And he did, and it did. It cost me big because I had a nervous breakdown.

"It was at that point and thereafter that the beauty and dignity of my mom and dad as their lives related to the

Scriptures began piecing themselves together. You could play many psychological games with my breakdown, relating it to Mom's fear and Dad's sense of inferiority and many things that were said, but in a very real way, I'm perturbed at the way we tend to want to heap blame on our parents for everything that's happened to us. One of the prophets said thousands of years ago, 'No longer shall it be said in Israel that the fathers have eaten sour grapes and the children's teeth are set on edge.' Let me say this, I don't care what sour grapes my dad ate, it's not my responsibility to say, 'Well, that's why my teeth are set on edge!' I am finally responsible for myself. I've got to keep myself in the equation.

"I'm convinced that good parents are, at one level, those whose children have taken responsibility for being stewards of their own lives. I'm a weak and hurting person. I still struggle with some of my mother's fear about conditional love—how could God love me? I still get a little angry with my dad. But then I fall back on the Word of God and the power of the gospel as it was worked out in Mom and Dad's life and how I hope it's being worked out in my life. That's how I tie in with my parents. Their faith had a genuineness that came through."

Did Harold Best have good parents? He says yes. He doesn't pretend they didn't have flaws. He doesn't pretend they didn't make mistakes, that he didn't rebel against them in a significant way. But he has wisely chosen to focus on what they did right instead of what they did wrong. And he keeps himself in the equation. He admits that what he considered at the time to be weaknesses on his parents' part, may have actually been his own weakness—an inability to receive the gifts they were trying to give him. "Did I sometimes miss what they were trying to give me?" he asks himself. "Did I sometimes misconstrue what they were trying to do?"

Maybe he did, at least during certain periods of his life. Maybe some of the people who are doing so much complaining about their parents these days have, in part, misunderstood their parents' intentions. And maybe, despite your sincerest efforts to do all the right things, your children will misconstrue what you're trying to do. Maybe they'll perceive your encouragement as pressure. Maybe they'll feel strangled by your love. Maybe they'll resent what seems to you to be reasonable discipline and healthy responsibility. Perhaps they'll reject the community with which you've surrounded them and the spiritual values in which you've immersed them. Maybe they won't appreciate the time you spend with them, the marriage you lived out in front of them, or the safety you offered them. Maybe they'll say the atmosphere you thought was so positive was really negative. Maybe, despite all your efforts to give them reason to be proud of you, they'll act as if they're embarrassed to be seen with you at certain times in their lives.

It could happen. Because, as a parent, you're only part of the equation. Your children can choose what to do with what you've given them, and it's possible that they'll choose to cast their upbringing in a negative light. The current tendency to wallow in tales of various forms of "toxic" parenting is proof of that.

But what has impressed me over and over in talking with people from many different backgrounds is the amazing capacity children seem to have for understanding their parents' motives. Parents who deeply love their children, sincerely want the best for them, and who attempt to act on those motivations, generally succeed. Their kids may not like everything their parents do, but they somehow understand at a very deep level the tenderness that their parents have toward them in their hearts. And, as my friend said, that goes a long way.

There are no clear markers between good, mediocre, and bad parents. Most of us are strong in some areas and weak in others. The picture of the "good parents" I've attempted to describe in these pages is actually a composite, a compilation of the qualities grown children said they appreciated about their parents.

What encourages me, as an all-too-flawed parent, is the fact that so many grown children were willing to rise up and call their parents blessed despite their failings.

I want to be a good parent. I want my children to rise up someday and call me blessed. The stories and reflections and insights shared by these grown children of unusually effective parents have inspired me and given me models to emulate. They've given me hope that someday my children will be able to look back and know that I tried to do my best—that someday they'll focus on my strengths and forgive me for my weaknessses.

My hope is that these stories will not only help you to do that for your parents, but also to raise your children in ways that will help them do that for you.